The Wake Up Call

The Wake Up Call

S.K. Trew

Copyright ©2017 by S.K. Trew

All rights reserved. This book or any portion thereof may not be reproduced or used in any manner whatsoever without the express written permission of the publisher except for the use of brief quotations in a book review.

Printed in the United States of America

First Printing, 2017

ISBN-13: 978-1-945949-13-5 print edition
ISBN-13: 978-1-945949-14-2 ebook

Waterside Press
2055 Oxford Ave
Cardiff, CA 92007
www.waterside.com

The Wake Up Call

S.K. Trew

Copyright ©2017 by S.K. Trew

All rights reserved. This book or any portion thereof may not be reproduced or used in any manner whatsoever without the express written permission of the publisher except for the use of brief quotations in a book review.

Printed in the United States of America

First Printing, 2017

ISBN-13: 978-1-945949-13-5 print edition
ISBN-13: 978-1-945949-14-2 ebook

Waterside Press
2055 Oxford Ave
Cardiff, CA 92007
www.waterside.com

Acknowledgements

I would like to give my heartfelt Thanks to Waterside productions and Bill Gladstone, for their kindness, patience, and encouragement. My first experience as a new Author has been scary, but with the help of Bill Gladstone and Kenneth it has been made so much easier, and I know I wouldn't of published this book without your help. I will be forever grateful to you.

I also would like to thank my dear friend Natalie Crabb for the amazing illustrations. I loved them from the very first sketch. You have a amazing gift to capture the content of my book and put it into pictures. I love you x.

And finally to my amazing Family and Friends, Thank you from my Soul, for believing in me long before I believed in myself.

Thank you for pushing me out of my comfort zone and encouraging me to send it to Agents, I wouldn't be here writing this without your support.

This one is for you, I love you always x.

Chapter One
An Urgent Meeting

Merlin called all the Angels for a meeting. Merlin was a very wise and respected member of the Angel Realm and rarely intervened with the Angels work. However, the time had come to ask the Angels for help with Planet Earth and the people who reside there.

As all the Angels and Archangels assembled in the Great Halls of Knowledge, the loud chatter of wonder about what Merlin wanted soon became whispers and then eventually silence. Merlin entered the hall and smiled at all of them. He then stood in the middle of the Hall, opened his hands and said

"Welcome", he then continued to say "I have asked you all to attend this meeting as a matter of urgency." A few whispers from the young Angels and then it was quiet once again.

Merlin carried on. "I need the young recruits to really pay attention to what I am about to say".

The young recruits are Angels that are learning about life on the Earth plane and what their role is, between Earth and the Angel Realm, and how they can sometimes help. They are aged between 11 years old and 60+ years old. Although this age is for the benefit of the Earth people, so they can connect. In the Angel Realm you don't have age, only how old your soul is. Old souls who have completed many lifetimes and have learnt knowledge, can choose to become Angels and Guides. Archangels are those who are there to help Angels and Guides and sometimes intervene and help the human beings from the Earth plane.

Merlin continued "Earth has become a very dark place and humans have been losing hope. This saddens me deeply. There is a dark force joining them and it is spreading darkness all over the earth. War is continuing, people are dying needlessly, people are suffering and worst of all, the new generation of crystal children are being supressed. So now it is time to intervene. Earth has been in a place of darkness for years. The Crystal Children were born, to bring light into the world, but they are now losing strength to continue the fight. This cannot continue. We will lose Planet Earth if we do not do something. Mother Earth has been crying out for years and we have tried our best to help, without getting too involved. However, the time has come for change and we are going to intervene!"

"Are you asking us to go and fight the darkness Merlin?" Archangel Michael asked questioningly.

"No I am not, violence and fighting is not the way forward, Archangel Michael, and you should know me better than that my friend."

"Yes I do, it's just the way you were talking…"

"No, I have a plan!" Merlin winked. "The Crystal Children are so aware when they first incarnate but by the time they are of teenage years, they start to lose their ability as life sucks them in and they follow their elders' beliefs and behaviour patterns. By the time they reach their 20's all but a few have lost their light and all hope is lost so there is no hope to give. This needs to change. We have so many Angels and Bringers of Light already residing on the Earth plane, and they have made a difference, but they are looked upon as unique, special, gifted people, but the Earth people are looking at these "Earth Angels" in the wrong way. The Messengers of Light have been misinterpreted. Earth people need to know that each and every one of them are unique, special and gifted, no matter of what race, creed, colour or religion they are. Each and every one of them can make a difference and can make the world a better place. Earth people can do wonderful, amazing things too. They all have a light within them that has been hidden by the dark, it has never stopped burning, it's there still shining, but no one can see it as it has been hidden behind walls of fear, self doubt and hate. They live in an illusion and have forgotten they even have a light."

"Life has damaged them and they have learned to hide their light and build walls of solid matter around them and they believe that this protects them from hurt, pain and hides their sensitivity and vulnerability. They are living a huge lie. An illusion which over the centuries has just got bigger."

A stir of whispers again in the Hall.

"However", Merlin continued, "the People of the Earth (light) are now just beginning to wake up as the People of the Dark are losing their strength, the people of the Dark are dying out, getting weaker and will eventually become extinct. The People of the Light are starting to fight back, wake up, and are now asking many questions, like 'is this it?' 'is this all there is to my life?' People of the Light are waking up to the fact that this way is no longer working and they are suffering and struggling unnecessarily. The People of the Light are now able to spread their light and connect to other people's light which has been hidden and, therefore, wake up the Light People and show them there is another way."

"The People of the Dark are not liking this light movement and are now becoming fearful and are fighting more than ever to suck the Light People back into the illusion and sadly sometimes they succeed."

"This is why I have summoned this meeting with you and I have especially asked for our young recruits to pay attention. It is you young recruits who are the ones who are going to take the lead on Planet Earth and become Bringers of the Light and show the People of the Light the way forward. You will be the ones to show them courage and self love and give them the confidence to show their light, this is their time to shine. You will encourage them to shine"

The Hall became noisy again with excited chatter.

"But!" Merlin shouted over the noise, "this is not a game, you will need to be very gentle and kind as well as very aware, because the People of the Light have been hidden from the Light for many centuries and they are only now just starting to wake up to the fact that what they have been living for all these centuries has been an illusion. That on its own is enough to send any human being crazy which is why so many Light People end up with mental health problems and depression, which is just where the People of the Dark want them.

"These people are known as the lost lights and we may never get them back. Some lost lights wake up too fast and the information they have received has become too much for them to understand. The light overwhelmed them, so they have became mentally ill. Therefore, we have to accept that we have lost them. Our job is to make sure they can live as comfortably as possible until it is their time to pass over and they can heal their light on a better level. Some, however, we can help". Merlin smiled.

"So our young recruits have to realise that this is a serious matter and their job is not to be taken lightly. You are all going to have to be careful not to blind them with your light and reality. They are going to be fearful of you, distrustful, and cautious. They are not going to accept that what you say is truth, however simple that truth may be. Remember, human beings have lived with complications for centuries and have the belief that nothing is simple."

"The People of the Light will be guarded, defensive and attacking. They will challenge you, question you, laugh at you, and belittle you, even humour you. You may even lose them for a while, as they go back to what they know and what they think and believe is 'safe' back there. Back there in the illusion is comfortable for them, because they have lived it for so long. This is normal for them. Remember my friends, they have been living their illusion for many, many years, and this illusion has been their reality. The truth is hard for them to see."

"So, to all the young recruits that are now feeling that they are not up to the job, be honest, we will find another job for you. By turning this mission down, you will not have failed. This mission is not a test. This mission is not an easy one, it will be dangerous and it will also teach you lots about yourself. You will, without a shadow of doubt, be attacked, judged, ridiculed and challenged. Sometimes you may even lose yourself, forget who you really are, and get sucked into their illusion. You may just start being judgemental, and attacking others, as well as being fearful."

"This is the hardest mission I have ever asked you young recruits to ever do. This mission will be the hardest test to remain TRUE TO YOURSELF AT ALL TIMES!. Regardless of how others are behaving or how strong the negative energy is pulling you in. Remember you are light and love and this energy will always be the strongest."

"Therefore, this mission is not for the faint hearted. I cannot express how tough this mission will be for you all. We, here, will be aware of each and every one of you and will call you home, when you are seen to be struggling or getting weak. We will always be on hand to help, all you have to do is ask and we will be there. We will always have your back, we will support you while you are helping others find their light."

"Whenever, you need to be reminded of who you really are, and that you are not walking this journey alone, we will send you a message, such as a white feather, pennies, a robin, the words in a song, hearts or numbers."

"Once this mission is over and we have succeeded, in spreading the love and light to other light people and giving them the courage to shine, the ramifications are endless!" The excited chatter in the Hall gets louder.

"Ok", Merlin says, trying to calm the young recruits down.

"As I have said before, the mission is hard, and there is a long journey ahead. I now want you to go and think about whether you want to sign up for this mission. Think long and hard and remember this is not part of a game, this is a mission. So I am giving you 48 hours to process this information and start to think about whether you want to do this mission. Don't rush, really think long and hard and discuss with your friends but make no firm decision just yet, because I will call you back for another meeting with more information in 48 hours time."

Archangel Michael speaks "Er, so what are we going to be doing while our young are on their mission?"

Merlin turns to look over at Michael with a wry smile and says "Michael my dear friend we have a bigger mission going on, right here on the Astral Planes. We are being called to protect these Astral Plaines, from the dark people who want ownership of all the Astral Planes. We have to try and maintain balance. Our Universe cannot survive in pure darkness."

"The People of the Dark want all control, all power, and own the Universe. They can not be allowed to succeed, because if they do the Universe will indeed implode and once again we will have nothing. For the sake of mankind on the Earth Planet and others that reside in the

Universe and on the Astral Planes and different dimensions, we need to intervene now! Before it's too late".

"Merlin, what do you mean when you say the Universe will implode once again, we will have nothing? Are you saying this has happened before and we didn't succeed?" Michael asked.

"Yes Michael, long ago, there was a war in the Universe, amongst the Gods, all fighting over ownership and power. This war was one that could never be won and the only way to end it was for the universe to implode in on itself."

"There was so much energy and at varying strengths, eventually all this energy coming from the Gods had to implode to create calm, however by doing this, it caused destruction of planets and the whole Universe became a black hole. This was the way it was for billions of years, until eventually once again the black hole exploded, scattering energy outwards once again, and a new Universe was created. During the time of the black hole, we didn't exist, we were just energy. When the black hole finally exploded, the rush of energy was intense, but more importantly new worlds were created."

"This time around we can all work together and not create another black hole. This is why our mission will be more dangerous Michael. If we push the People of the Dark too far we will become nothing once again. This is a fight for existence. This cannot be the end. We need the People of the Light to wake up the Earth Plane to assist us. The love of power has to cease and the power of love has to succeed. Once the Light People wake up, we will have more love and we can succeed in saving our Universe and other beings who reside there."

"Once we have achieved this, we can help other beings and planets. This my dear friend, is only the beginning."

"So, are we going to extinguish the dark, you know get shot of it, fight to the death!" Archangel Michael says in his once again ready for battle voice.

Merlin chuckled "No Michael, this battle is not about winning or losing or dying or living, this mission is about bringing balance back into the Universe. We cannot exist without the dark and the dark cannot exist without the light, we need opposites always. It's the law of the

Universe. This is a mission to stop the dark from taking over, because if they succeed, we will implode once again, and the sad thing is, the People of the Dark don't believe that will happen. They now believe that they can take over the whole Universe and continue to exist. Their own power will destroy them as well as us. The People of the Dark have built in confidence as they have already achieved so much on the Earth Plane. If they are allowed to continue, they will destroy the Earth Plane, hence why our young recruits need to go and live amongst them, and show the Light People how to shine. Our mission is to stop the People of the Dark in and around the Astral Planes and the Universe, spreading their dark light."

"We have to have dark forces as they are our natural opposites and our universe is all about balance. However, over the centuries the dark forces have invaded Planet Earth, and have gained power and control. This has to change and bring Planet Earth back into balance."

"As the dark forces evolved they were able to bring fear into the People of the Light. Dark forces built up their power so strongly that the Light People didn't feel strong enough to fight and fear took over and the Light People were forced to become dark like them. They started out by hiding their light, building walls of solid matter around them to protect themselves. They stopped feeling 'them' to protect themselves. They stopped feeling the unconditional love that was vibrating through them, which in turn left the Light People unable to have unconditional love for all those that resided on this beautiful planet. Instead the Light People, under the dark forces influence, judged others, put others down, and most of all learned how to hate. Greed, Power, Illusion became the leaders of this planet and to survive the Light People became the same."

"Over the years religion became the light and the Earth People slowly followed religion, but even religion had rules and commandments. Eventually the People of the Dark managed to portray themselves as Light People and do good for others, but this was not genuine and certainly not unconditional, but it worked. Our Light People learned from the People of the Dark that this way would always give you what you wanted, but when it didn't you would curse the other, judge the other, and spread hate to the other. Now the time has come to bring back balance."

"Ok, I now want you to go away, think about what I've asked of you all and then I will call you back for another meeting."

There was a rumble of movement and loud chatter as the Angels started to leave the Hall. Merlin watched with caution, for he knew that some would not be up for the job, but trusted that they would make the right decision.

As the Halls of Knowledge became empty and quiet, Merlin noticed an Angel still sitting right at the back. He walked over to her and asked her if she was ok. She looked up at Merlin and stared into his amazing blue eyes, she then nodded and looked back down at her feet.

Merlin sat down beside her and gently said "What's troubling you?"

Still staring at the floor, she replied "I really want to help, really I do, but I'm really scared."

"That's totally understandable to be really scared. That's why the decision cannot be made with haste, what is it that you are scared of?"

The young Angel looked up at Merlin, with wide eyes and whispered "being judged, looking foolish, feeling vulnerable, feeling alone, being attacked for what we are trying to do."

"My dear Angel, these are normal and these fears are already in those human beings already residing on the Earth Plane. Can I ask you another question?"

"Sure"

"Are you scared of giving without getting? Loving without being loved? Trusting without being trusted? Doing your best for others, without getting others best for you? Remaining true to yourself and your beliefs?"

Without any hesitation the young Angel replied "No not at all."

"Even if it means you do get hurt and disappointed at times by others?"

"Even if I get hurt and disappointed by others, I will never be scared of any of the giving without getting."

"Then I believe that you will do excellently on the Earth Plane and for those who do judge you, attack you, abuse your love and trust, they will fade out of your life and you will attract more Earth Angels who are on the same mission as you. Your mission is to wake up those who need to know they have a light and they do matter. People will be drawn to you by your light, but your job is to show them their light".

"However, I repeat, this will not be easy and you will be challenged. You will be challenged and judged by the people who claim to be spiritual, loving people too. This can cause you disappointment and pain, but remember these people are coming from a place of ego and ego creates a competitive, jealous, envious nature. These spiritual people also have fears and insecurities, and may also not realise they are living in an illusion."

"These people are spiritual and are trying to do good and share their light but unfortunately they get sucked in to the ego and then find themselves in an illusion. They may be spiritual and talk it, but they need to now walk it. Drop the ego, drop the competition, jealousy and envy, live love, be love and shine your light no matter what."

"You are already evolved, you already shine your light. You already love unconditionally and give without getting. The people of the Earth are scared of exactly the same as you, they are scared of being vulnerable, being judged, feeling alone, the difference is they also are scared of giving without getting. Loving without being loved, trusting without being trusted, doing their best for others, even though others do not do their best for them. They get hurt and damaged by life and others. So what happens is they build a hard exterior barrier around them so they cannot get hurt anymore, and then become that hard and then forget the beautiful light that now is hidden underneath. There are a few beautiful lights on the Earth plane, trying to shine for others to see, but at present, they are remaining hopeful of the world becoming a beautiful place and remaining true to themselves by not conforming to the Earth People's ugly ways. They are keeping hold of their dreams while the People of the Earth let go of theirs. They are keeping their inner child alive while others lose theirs in the waves of life, but this is becoming more and more difficult for them because of the dark force."

"This is why I have called on you and your fellow Angels. This is urgent and we need to intervene not with violence but with more light and more love. My dear Sophia, you have such wisdom and knowledge, you will be a great but quiet force on the Earth Plane and I know you will do absolutely wonderful things on this mission. Because you come from love. You know, I had the same fear, when I discovered I had wisdom and knowledge that no one else had and I found I had a magical side to me too. In fact, I was actually scared of that side of me I feared it, so I pushed it away for a long time. But it never went, it kept coming back. So I had to accept it and love it and learn about it and eventually the fear went and I did good things."

Merlin smiled, but his thoughts took him back to when he feared the gifts he was given and boy was he scared. Merlin shook his head to clear the thoughts and looked at Sophia and spoke gently.

"Sophia, it is ok to be fearful, because the opposite of fear is courage and remember to have courage isn't because the fear has left, courage is triumph over it. Now go, rest, no more thinking, just allow yourself some rest. I know you will make the right decision. Trust yourself my dear Sophia". Merlin stood up and walked away.

Sophia took a deep breath in and blew out hard as she stood up, trying to release this feeling of fear. Deep in her thoughts – no more thinking, Merlin says, trust yourself, Merlin says! Oh my goodness! It's not that easy… Feeling confused and uncertain Sophia walked back to her room.

Chapter Two
Choices

There was a knock on Merlin's big wooden door, Merlin opened the door, "Mother Mary I've been expecting you, please do come in".

Mother Mary is the Queen of all the Angels and the blessed in Heaven. She has great humility, compassion and empathy. Mother Mary has the power to assign missions to the Saints and Angels. Mother Mary is strong but kind. She rules the good Angels and controls the bad. Mother Mary has the last word on all Angel's missions. She is their protector and will protect them with all of her will. Mother Mary knows how hard this mission will be and has fought in missions like it many times before. The safety of her Angels is her main priority.

"Hello Merlin", Mother Mary smiled as she entered.

Merlin's home was very homely and the energy of the place would put anyone at ease. Although he has wall to wall bookshelves filled with all sorts of books, knowledge and wisdom, the room is tidy and spacious with comfy sofas and soft lighting on small wooden tables. There is an open fire and although not lit yet there was still last night's burnt ash and remnants of a log in it, and the smell of pine was faint but still noticeable.

Merlin smiled "Ok let's get straight to the mission itself, who do you think is not ready to complete this mission?"

"Well" Mother Mary paused before she spoke again. "I believe we will have a few thousand that we need to stay here and guard our home and they will all already know who they are. However there are 9 of our young recruits who I would like to stay here, as I believe they will help here more than on Earth. It's not that I do not believe in them or their ability but I believe they will be more useful here, and to watch over our Heavens."

Merlin nodded his head in agreement. "So, who are they? We need to let them know as soon as possible so they do not feel too disappointed."

"Ok well, there is Pabel, Penac, Shlomeil, Sehiah, Fraigne, Drialo, Calvel, Bernal, and finally Abedumabal."

Merlin frowned "Mmm forgive me for asking, but Abedumdaal? Why? I would have thought he would have been a great recruit for the mission after all he is the Angel of Magical prayer".

Mother Mary smiled "I understand why you would think that Merlin, but the reason for him to stay is so he can watch over our young recruits and the ones seen to be struggling he can send a message through his prayers to bring comfort to them. He can send them white feathers or coins, hearts or songs on the radio, he can even send numbers to let them know, we are still with them. He will be able to send them these signs so they know that they are not alone. Merlin there are going to be thousands of young recruits on Earth needing him to send a sign at different stages of their mission. Whereas if he were to be on the Earth with them, he will only be able to reach and help those that are in the same area as him. Being here, he can help and comfort all of them."

Merlin chuckled, "Yes you are right as usual, I can see that now, excellent shall we call them in?"

"Yes we can, but let's not do it yet, I have a feeling they will come to us."

"Ok, so what are we going to do with any other recruits who don't feel they are up to the mission?"

"Merlin, that will be your job to convince them they are, I believe that they will all be excellent lightworkers, the only thing that will stop them is fear, but they are more than capable of doing great work, they just need to have belief in themselves, and the only way of knowing they can do this, is for them to do it, experience it and evolve from it, so they then can teach the next generation of young recruits. This is their calling."

Merlin stood up from his chair and began to walk around the room, gazing at his thousands of books lining the walls, but which strangely enough did not look cluttered or messy.

"What else is bothering you Merlin" Mother Mary asked.

"The bigger battle on the Astral Planes…"

Just then there was a knock on the door.

"Come in" Merlin turned to look at the door and in came Angels Pabel and Penac. Pabel spoke first.

"Er, we have both come together as we were talking about this mission and both felt that we would be better staying here, to watch over the heavens and the recruits I mean…"

Mother Mary and Merlin looked at each other with a knowing smile.

Merlin replied "Yes we know what you mean, Pabel, Mother Mary and I agree."

"You do?" Penac said with slight relief in his voice.

"Yes" Mother Mary replied "and your job will be just that, to watch over our young recruits and send them energy while they are there, but also to watch over this place, it's going to be fairly empty for a while and you will be guarding and protecting it from harm. This is your job, Guardians of the Angelic Realm. You won't be the only ones being called to watch over this Realm, you will be with others. They just haven't come forward as yet."

"Thank you Mother Mary" Pabel and Penac said in unison, and both turned and walked out of the room.

"Merlin I've got to go and speak with some younger recruits but we will talk more about our bigger battle soon."

"Yes, ok, speak soon." Merlin replied still deep in thought.

Back outside in the Gardens of Cherubs, most of the young recruits were talking amongst themselves and discussing the mission. The feeling of excitement was still in the air. On his own, a young recruit Zeruch Angel of Strength (known to his friends as Zee), sat under a cherry blossom tree. He wasn't scared of the mission ahead, he had been waiting for this moment. This would enable him to show his strength, not with anger or aggression but with courage, humility and love. The challenge for Zee was not to allow the ego in. Zee was well liked and very popular with all the young Angels. However, he sometimes got attached to his ego and became a big head with arrogance. He had been working really hard on himself to not allow his ego invade who he really was. This mission was going to be tough for him, but he was willing to take it on.

He sat trying to focus on his strength and positivity breathing in the light and repeating the positive affirmation. "I shall remain true to myself, I am safe, all is well."

"Ah there you are", Mother Mary said. "I've been looking for you, we need to talk". Zee jumped up for the tree, rubbing the dirt off his trousers, and walked towards Mother Mary.

"We need to talk?" Zee asked questioningly.

"Yes" Mother Mary smiled. "But don't look so worried, it's nothing bad." Zee took a deep sigh, "Cool" he said.

"How are you feeling about this mission Zee?"

"Erm, yes I feel good about it, can't wait in fact, I'm ready or I feel ready" Zee replied excitedly.

There was a long pause as they continued walking around the Cherub Gardens. Other recruits smiled as they walked past.

Mother Mary spoke "Zee, I am very proud of the hard work you have done on yourself and I have every faith you will be a successful candidate for the mission ahead."

"Why thank you Mother Mary, I'm…."

"But I have my concerns for you." Mother Mary looked directly at Zee with a serious look on her face. Zee stopped talking and looked back at her.

Mother Mary continued "This mission is going to be difficult for you Zee. It's easy working on yourself here, you have, help, guidance, support, encouragement and love at all times. You are also surrounded by other recruits who are on the same wavelength, and path as you. You can only be influenced by the people around you, so there is only success and never failure. There is no such thing as failure here Zee, just feedback."

"You know we show you where you are going and try to help guide you back to the more positive path, and you understand and see clearly what way you were going and you change it. This has been great for you and this is why you have grown and evolved so much quicker and you have a passion for it."

"I do very much want to do this mission Mother Mary, I want to take all my knowledge and share it with the Light People." Zee said more softly.

"Zee I know you do, and I know you can do it i think my concern is once you arrive on the Earth Plane, it is very different to here, very different! Knowledge, my dear Zee, is all very well and good, but putting that knowledge into practice and actually living it always, is so much harder and now it will be even harder to live your truth and knowledge once on the Earth Plane. I have concerns that you will get sucked into their way of life, you are sensitive Zee and are easily influenced by others".

"Me sensitive?" Zee exclaimed.

Mother Mary chuckled "Yes sensitive Zee, you just hide it well, but I see you, and who you really are and you are definitely a sensitive young Angel."

"Mmm maybe, although I'm not sure I agree with you, I never saw myself as sensitive!"

Mother Mary smiled, "And that is why I have my concerns, there is still lots for you to learn about yourself, and still lots to work on, but this mission is urgent and we don't have more time to waste. So all we can do is give you as much knowledge and guidance before you all set off on this mission."

"We need your wisdom too Mother Mary, knowledge may not be enough".

"Zee, I cannot give you wisdom, wisdom comes from yourself. You can have knowledge, but not actually really know, you can only gain wisdom through the experience of knowledge".

"I'm not sure I understand what you mean Mother Mary."

Mother Mary smiled softly and her face softened and she changed from her serious talking to use a softer tone.

"Ok, let me explain, Merlin has told you all, about this mission, he has said this mission will not be an easy one. He has also warned that this mission is not a game and not to be taken lightly. Merlin also said this mission is going to be a tough mission and a test for you all to remain true to yourselves. This is knowledge he is giving you, but you will never really know whether this knowledge is true knowledge or knowledge from another person's experience. So only when you get to the Earth Plane will you truly know whether Merlin's knowledge is true for you. Once you experience and live through the knowledge given to you, will you truly know and then you will have the wisdom."

"Another example for you, I have told you that you are a sensitive person and my concern for you is that you may get influenced by the People of the Dark and forget who you really are, but you are quite sure you are not sensitive and you won't get sucked into their life. You see from where you are standing in life, right now you have a knowing that is strong and you are quite sure you will not get sucked in. However, you will not really know for sure until you have experienced life on the Earth Plane and then you will have wisdom. That is when you can truly say I know this mission is not an easy one or Merlin was right in what he told us. You would have the wisdom not just knowledge. Wisdom comes with knowledge, knowledge comes from experience."

"I understand now Mother Mary, thank you for helping me. Does Merlin have the wisdom because he has already lived through this knowledge?" Zee asked.

"Merlin has experienced so much and lots of different missions, which is where he gets his knowledge through his wisdom, there is a very deep, gentle, sensitive soul within Merlin, but he very rarely shows this to anyone. We go to Merlin, for his wisdom, knowledge, magic and his sense of humour, however there is more to Merlin than meets the eye", Mother Mary drifted off, as if she was remembering something.

Shaking her head, she continued, "Anyway, here we are, back to the present and the mission ahead, I'm glad we talked Zee, please think about what we have spoken about, I have to go but will see you again soon".

"Sure I will, and thank you again, bye" replied Zee. Zee turned and walked back to the cherry blossom, deep in thought, not sure he was ready after all.

Back in her room Sophia was trying not to think too much about the mission ahead, but was finding it hard to let it go, but her thoughts were broken by a knock on the door.

"Oh hey", smiled Sophia "You ok?"

"Yeah, sighed Jazz "Well no not really, but I'll be ok."

"I know the feeling" said Sophia in a low tone.

"I'm sorry for disturbing you, I don't even know why I've come to you, I mean we don't really know each other do we?"

"No we don't, but it's ok, you have done me a favour, you coming has got me out of over thinking so thank you for that." Sophia replied, relieved.

Jazz smiled and then said "Oh dear, I think I may spoil your clear head, I came to ask what you had decided to do or whether you had any inclination of which choice to make. You see all my friends are so eager to do this mission but I'm quite scared, but I can't share that with them, as they will think I've lost it. I'm usually the loud one and the action one and don't really fear anything and…."

"I know who you are Jazz, I've watched you in action." Sophia laughed, "Look it is ok to be scared, we just have to decide whether we believe and trust ourselves enough to remain true to ourselves and not be tempted by the People of the Dark, but also be strong enough to try to help wake up the Light People. I know I want to help, but I'm not sure I can or will be able to cope with the mission ahead. Merlin's words scared me, I mean he was serious, this is not one of our tasks or one of our lessons, this is a very real mission."

"Oooo you see, that's what I mean, I get shivers when I think about it like that, but I still want to do it, but I want to be with someone who will help me if I get lost or caught up with the People of the Dark. I know I will need that support, but my friends are just finding it more exciting than scary and to them it's like a big adventure and as much as I want to be with them, I've watched you from afar, I know you will be the one to take this seriously." Jazz looked deep into Sophia's eyes. Sophia could feel Jazz's desperation and enthusiasm for the mission ahead but could also sense her vulnerability and sensitivity and warmed to her.

Jazz was another young recruit, but she was quite loud and always ready for action. She was also a great leader and was always willing to learn, she had a thirst for knowledge and took her tasks and lessons seriously. She always managed to get further than anyone else and her tasks and lessons were always marked at the top.

Jazz used her energy to take her forward, but underneath the energy of action her true self was of a sensitive, vulnerable, shy and sometimes fearful young Angel. Other young recruits believed they knew Jazz, but they would never see the sensitive, vulnerable shy and sometimes fearful side, as Jazz always hid that side away. Jazz, herself didn't feel comfortable with that side of herself, so she wasn't about to show anyone who she truly was.She even shortened her name from Jasmine to Jazz, shying away from her real self. Although Sophia knew her, she saw who she was. The thought of this mission excited her, although the feelings of fear and failure unnerved her much to her surprise as she didn't think she had ever experienced these feelings before, which is why she found herself knocking on Sophia's door.

Sophia is a quiet, deep, observant, sensitive young angel, but she is much more than that. She has patience, compassion, understanding and empathy for others, in fact she is one of the more evolved young Angels and other Angels often would go to her for her wise council. Sophia never seemed to get angry or frustrated and if she did, you would never see it. She is always willing to help others, but her love is working and looking after the Cherubs and the Cherubs were always drawn to her.

Sophia has the ability to calm, comfort and make you feel safe, from Cherub to young Angels they all love Sophia and want to be around her all the time.

Sophia's drawback is that she doesn't trust many and more importantly doesn't trust herself or believe in herself. Her fear holds her back much to Merlin's frustration. Sophia doesn't feel good enough and has a genuine fear of failure which is why Merlin wants her to do this mission as she will learn so much about herself and most importantly learn to trust and believe in herself. Her fear of how others view her disables her belief in herself. She fears looking stupid or foolish, she fears betrayal and also being judged, so this genuine fear stops her from growing and evolving. Although she is happy to be where she is, it is very much her comfort zone, she feels safe here. This mission however, if she accepts it, will be her biggest test yet and she won't be able to stop herself from evolving. When she stops worrying about how others view her, and she starts to trust and believe in herself she will fly.

Sophia smiled warmly "Jazz, bless you for your faith in me, I am taking it seriously, but still I am not sure whether I'm actually ready for this mission."

"You have gotta be kidding me Sophia, you were made for this mission!!" Jazz exclaimed.

Sophia laughed a little nervously "Jazz, I'm flattered by your faith in me, I really am, but I do need to think about this seriously and not make hasty decisions I may regret."

"I totally understand where you are at Sophia, but I really don't know if I can do this, knowing you won't be there." Jazz replied with a sadness in her voice.

"I am certain you Jazz, will be just fine without me, you were made for this mission. You are a great leader and get stuck in to any of the tasks that are given to you, you will be absolutely fab at it, I have no doubt and also there are no guarantees we will even be in the same area, we may go through this whole mission never actually meeting, now how scary is that thought?"

"Uh huh, I will ask Mother Mary for us to be stationed near each other, I'm sure she will understand our fears, and say we can be in the same area."

"Mmm" muttered Sophia "we will see."

"Well I'm going to see if I can find Mother Mary and ask her; hey thanks for the chat." smiled Jazz and opened the door and left.

Suddenly Sophia was once again left with all of her thoughts. "Argh I really don't know!" exclaimed Sophia out loud.

Back in the Cherubs Garden there was excited chatter of young Angels discussing the mission and whether they were going to do it or not.

Zee was still under the cherub tree, but was now deep in conversation with Nathalie another young recruit who was uncertain on whether to do this mission. There was so much to take on board and Merlin's talk was to be taken seriously.

Abedumabal known to his friends as Abe, was walking through the Cherub Gardens, on his way to find Merlin. After deep consideration, he has made a decision not to do the mission, he feels he would be more help staying here.

"Hey Abe!" Zee shouted over the chatter of young Angels.

Abe looked over and waved, Zee waved him to go over. Abe started walking over towards Zee, thinking to himself that whatever Zee said, he would stick to his decision.

"Hi!" Abe said as he got closer and nodded to acknowledge Nathalie who was also with Zee.

"So have you made a decision yet or are you going to wait to hear more information at the next meeting?" Zee asked Abe.

"I've already made my decision, in fact that's where I was going when you called me over."

"To see Merlin?"

"Yes," Abe said "to find him and tell him I would like to stay here, I believe I will be of more help."

"Oh!" said Nathalie not quite understanding how he would be more help by staying. "Well fair play to you Abe, and I'm sure Merlin will find a job for you to do which will be just as important" Zee said without any sarcasm, surprisingly.

"Thanks Zee", replied Abe surprised by Zee's answer, "Anyway I best go and find Merlin and let him know."

"Cool, catch you around Abe."

"Yes, bye Abe and good luck with Merlin." said Nathalie.

Abe walked away quite relieved that Zee never made any attempt to change his mind.

Mother Mary was on her way back to Merlin to discuss the bigger battle on the Astral Planes. She knew he was aware of the fight ahead and once again he was in the place he was many eons ago and had no idea, where this battle was going to lead.

"Mother Mary" Jazz called out, breaking Mother Mary's thoughts.

"Oh hello Jazz, what is it?"

"Can we talk, in private please?" Jazz asked.

"Erm," she paused, thinking she really needed to see Merlin, but Jazz obviously needed to talk now.

"Ok, let's go into the Contemplation Garden, no one is there at the minute."

"Great!" Jazz said relieved that Mother Mary had time to talk.

The Contemplation Garden was small with a small pond and a water fountain in it. There are high hedges and trees, with lots of different colour flowers and shrubs, and a gravel path all the way round. There was also a large log cabin at the bottom with a veranda all around it. Inside this log cabin are two sofas at either end and scatter cushions everywhere. There are no books or tables or chairs in this cabin, and the garden is purely to contemplate and reflect. After the recruits have had lessons to learn or tasks that they have done, they come to this garden to reflect or contemplate. Sitting down on one of the sofas in the log cabin, Mother Mary said "So young Jazz, what did you want to speak to me about?"

"Well, you see, I really want to do this mission, and I believe it will teach me so much about myself. Also I would like to put into practice all that I have learned so far and to give back what I have been given, such as love, support and guidance. The fact that Planet Earth or the people need us to help them bring back balance makes me want to do it more."

"I see, so what's the problem?"

"The problem, Mother Mary, is I'm scared of doing it alone, and although my friends are all ready for the mission, and excited about it, I think I'm a bit more hesitant because I do fear being sucked in by the People of the Dark and their illusion and that bothers me big time! I feel I will need someone to pull me back to the light and somebody who will help me and work alongside me, but none of my friends understand that and think I will be great on Earth and I will be a great leader, which is lovely for them to say, but I don't feel that way at all. Merlin's meeting and the information he gave us, gives me shivers when I think about it".

"So what are you saying? Are you opting out of the mission?"

"No not at all, however, I have just been to see Sophia."

Mother Mary smiled "Ah yes Sophia."

"I went to see Sophia, to find out if she had made a decision, I mean I don't even know why I went to her, I don't really know her, but I've watched her from a distance and she is good, very good, but if you are not watching her, she goes unnoticed. I believe she will be better than me on this mission, I believe not only will she wake the Light People up, but also help her fellow Angels when they get lost, or sucked into the illusion of the dark."

"Mmm I totally agree with you Jazz."

"I would like to request that I am stationed near her on Earth, so I can perhaps find her or she find me, can we do that?"

"I'm not entirely sure Jazz, I will need to discuss it with Merlin, as to whether that can be arranged. What does Sophia want, does she want the same as you?" Mother Mary asked.

"Well this is why I needed to speak to you, you see I don't think Sophia wants to do this mission at all and she is still thinking about her decision and even though I've said to her, that I don't think I can do this mission without her being there also, she still really doesn't think she can do it. I even said I would ask you if we could be stationed together and all she said was "mmm we will see". I believe she would be so good on this mission and yet I don't think she believes that for herself, Mother Mary".

Mother Mary paused, she knew Sophia was ready for this mission. Sophia was one of the best, her intuition was spot on, her awareness, love, understanding and compassion were second to none. Mother Mary knew Sophia would help not only Jazz, but other young recruits plus help bring the Earth People back into balance.

"Jazz, you are right in what you say about Sophia, let me speak with Merlin and I will get back to you."

"Thank you so much Mother Mary" Jazz sighed relieved that she had spoken to Mother Mary.

"Go on now, it must be dinner time and you must be starving, I'll speak to you soon".

"Great, yes I am, and thank you once again". Jazz replied and walked out of the gardens.

Mother Mary stood up from the sofa and looked out of the cabin towards the Sea of Colour thinking to herself, that the talk with Merlin about the battle on the Astral Planes would have to wait. He will have to go and speak with Sophia, and try and convince her that she will be great on this mission. Stepping out of the cabin, Mother Mary made her way out of the garden. Mmm, I think I will have dinner first before speaking to Merlin.

The dinner hall was full of noisy, hungry, young recruits still discussing the mission and trying to make the right decision. Soon it fell quiet and all you could hear was the clatter of knives and forks and the young recruits appreciating the food and realising how hungry they were.

Merlin stayed in his room and had his dinner alone, he had been visited by Abe earlier and had a good talk with him about his decision to stay, and they discussed what Abe's duties would be.

Mother Mary finished dinner and retired to her room for the night. It had been a hectic day with so much activity all around her, Merlin would have to wait until tomorrow, he would understand. In fact, all of the recruits were off to bed for an early night. Apart from the odd whispers from the young recruits occasionally, the place fell silent.

The following morning, Mother Mary was feeling refreshed from a good night's sleep and was looking forward to catching up with Merlin and discussing Sophia with him. Sophia on the other hand, had a restless night and had not slept much at all. She finally woke at 5am and decided to get up, there was no point in getting frustrated and anxious about sleep any more.

Mother Mary found Merlin after breakfast in the Great Halls of Knowledge, looking out of the window on to the Cherub Gardens.

"Morning Merlin, did you sleep well?"

"Ah good morning, yes I did, thank you, yourself?"

"Yes, I needed to sleep, I feel so much better this morning." Mother Mary replied with a smile.

"Good, pleased to hear that, so what's the feeling you get amongst the young recruits?"

"Oh Merlin, that's why I've come to you this morning. I had Jazz visit me yesterday."

"Oh" said Merlin slightly surprised.

"Yes, she came to me with a bit of a dilemma, she really wants to do this mission but is quite scared, so apparently she went to see Sophia, to see if Sophia had made a decision about the mission."

"And?" Merlin questioned.

"Well Sophia is undecided, but Jazz told her that she couldn't do the mission without Sophia being there with her. Sophia told her there were no guarantees they would meet on the Earth Plane once they were there anyway, which is why Jazz came to me, to ask if there was any way they could be stationed in the same area. Personally Merlin I feel Sophia would be fantastic on this mission, so you may have to have a talk with her, we could make sure they meet up at some point in their lives even if it is for a short time, just to put Jazz back on the right track, and other recruits too, we could guide those that are losing their way to a recruit that has not forgotten why they are there, don't you think Merlin?"

"Yes, I don't see why they can't, excellent idea and if it helps others also get back to their mission, then so be it. I will try and speak with Sophia later, in the meantime I'm still a little concerned about the fight we have on the Astral Planes."

"Yes, I'm aware, something is troubling you Merlin, but I really need to go and organise some young recruits for their final task before they get ready for this mission, we will talk later."

"Yes, right you are, you best go and get organising, I'll be ok, but we do need to talk." Merlin replied looking over his reading glasses with raised eyebrows and a serious look.

Mother Mary smiled and left Merlin with his thoughts.

Chapter Three
Sophia the reluctant recruit

"Have you seen Sophia?" Merlin asked a group of young recruits just leaving the breakfast hall.

"Er no, I think she went back to her room" said one recruit shyly.

"Great, thank you!" Merlin made his way to her room, while Sophia made her way to the Great Halls of Knowledge, she felt she needed to contemplate in silence and not be distracted by noisy chatter.

Merlin knocked on Sophia's door, but had no answer, he then had a feeling she was in the Great Halls, and headed towards them.

Mother Mary managed to track down Jazz and told her about what Merlin and her had agreed on. Jazz was relieved and so much happier and she hoped that Merlin would be able to persuade Sophia into going.

Sophia sat on the window seat at the very end of the halls, looking out on to the grounds of this beautiful place she called home. She felt lucky to be here, she loved her home and all that resided there with her. She felt lucky to have such great teachers and felt humble towards them. Deep in thought about what she would be leaving behind if she decided to do the mission, she didn't notice Merlin walking towards her. He made her jump as he spoke.

"There you are."

"Oh Merlin, you made me jump!" Sophia exclaimed with a slight chuckle, not many people made Sophia jump.

"May I sit with you a while?"

"Of course Merlin." replied Sophia.

"So have you thought anymore about this mission Sophia?"

"Oh my, I haven't stopped thinking about this mission Merlin, in fact it's giving me a headache and my thoughts won't give me a break."

"What is it that is stopping you from making a choice?" Merlin asked gently.

"Fear mainly, it's like we talked about before, but it all boils down to fear, and I know sometimes you have to feel the fear and do it anyway, but that's easier said than done. I just don't feel like I'm up for this mission, I'm scared I will 'blend in' and not be noticed, because of fear of judgement, I'm not the sort of person who has confidence to be me, I know I will become that people pleaser so I'm liked. I feel so safe here, everyone knows me, and I don't have to people please, I am free to be me here and no one judges me, we are all one here."

"But Sophia, don't you see that's why your friends here want you to do this mission with them, they know you, understand you and feel they need you on this mission. They know you are ready and will be so good on this mission."

"Merlin, they are talking from here, it's going to be so different there, there won't just be People of the Light there, but People of the Dark too, and you said yourself that this mission is a very difficult one and we will be challenged. To be fair, Merlin I don't want to be challenged or confronted, I love being here, life is good. Merlin, I'm really struggling with this mission, I believe it's a hopeless one, I don't think all of us going to Earth will change anything, in actual fact I think we will be put at risk and not only lose the Light People, but lose ourselves as well. I'm just really scared Merlin, but also I think what is the point? Let the Universe implode, let the Universe decide what to do."

"Sophia! You don't have an understanding of what you are saying!" Merlin exclaimed despairingly.

"This is why the Earth is in the state it's in because People of the Earth, also feel hopeless and they are leaving the few people to make choices for them. If the Universe implodes, which it has done before, we won't exist, we will just go back to the source. We will be nothing but energy, we are not meant to be going backwards, we are meant to be evolving, moving forward. You cannot mean what you are saying Sophia, all that we have learnt, how much we have grown and evolved, we have come too far to go back to nothing but a mass of energy."

"There are scientists and researchers on Earth, who right now are finding out amazing things, they have just discovered there is no such thing as time and also that there are other planets with life forms out in the Universe, this my dear Sophia is evolvement moving forward. Medical science is evolving, there will be cures for diseases. Technology is evolving, moving forward, but at the same time the Earth has wars still going on and hate, poverty and greed, this is the People of the Dark. With the help of you and the young recruits we can bring the Earth back into balance and while you are all working on Earth, we will be working in the Universe and other planets. Sophia you must seriously consider doing this mission, you will be ok, you will help massively and you will feel so good for actually being a part of it."

"Merlin, I hear you and understand what you are saying but my feeling is not one of excitement but more of dread, and maybe that is fear, I just need more time."

"Ok, so be it, take all the time you need, my dear Sophia, I'm sure your decision will be the right one". Merlin stood up and gave her a knowing wink.

"I'm off now to speak to other recruits, but if you need to see me, I will be at mine after 2pm this afternoon."

"Thank you Merlin" Sophia answered quietly and as Merlin walked away, Sophia took a deep sigh and continued looking out of the window.

Sophia must have fallen asleep because she was woken by a gentle touch on her cheek and opened her eyes to see Zee standing over her. Zee really liked Sophia, she fascinated him, there was more to her than met the eye.

"Hey" he said softly "Are you comfy? You don't look comfy, come and sit on a comfy chair."

He held his hand out to help her, but she ignored it. Sophia moved without talking on to the big soft armchair, her arm and leg had gone dead and her arm was now tingling with pins and needles. Rubbing her arm to get circulation back into it, she realised she was not comfy.

She spoke to Zee "How long were you there before you woke me?"

"Oh long enough" Zee chuckled, knowing that Sophia would be embarrassed at being asleep in a public place for everyone to see.

"Oi!" Sophia said still in a sleepy tone. "If I had the energy I would give you a slap for being cheeky, but all this thinking has left me exhausted."

"Oh yeah, I know, I bumped into Merlin a little while ago and he told me you were still undecided about this mission."

"Did Merlin send you over to try and persuade me"? Sophia said, getting herself straight in the chair.

"Don't flatter yourself Soph, of course he didn't. No it's just my curiosity that brought me here, I want to know what's going on in that mind of yours?"

Sophia raised her eyebrows, looking at him she realised there was something about him that she quite liked, but she couldn't quite put her finger on it. He had nice hazel eyes and a great smile but it wasn't that, maybe it was his sense of humour, although sometimes he was arrogant and a bit cheeky, but there was definitely an attraction that she hadn't noticed before.

"What?" Zee asked.

"What?" Sophia replied.

"You're just staring at me not talking."

"Well," she replied stretching and yawning, "you will have to remain curious, because I don't want to talk about it or think about it anymore."

"Oh come on Soph, let us in, I just need your view on this mission." Zee replied with a hint of seriousness in his voice.

"Zee, get out of here you are not interested in anyone's view, you've already made your mind up that you are going on this mission."

"I am interested in your view Soph!" Zee said with a wink.

Sophia giggled, "Whatever!"

"Ah there you are, you have a great smile Soph, all that frowny frowny just doesn't suit you. For what it's worth, I do hope you come on this mission. I think you will be so good at reaching out to the People of the Light, I believe you will make a difference and damn, we, all of us will need someone like you with us, to help us too."

Standing up to go, Zee looked at Sophia in the eyes and said softly,

"I need someone like you there, to keep me on the straight and narrow; I hope you come." and with that said he turned and walked back down the halls, leaving Sophia in ponderous thought.

Archangel Michael was just finishing another task outside in the Cherub Gardens for the young recruits, when Merlin called him over. Archangel Michael jogged over to him.

"Hey Merlin, what's up?"

"Michael, I really need to get you all together to discuss the bigger battle we have going on, but need Mother Mary to be present too, it's important."

"Ok." Michael replied.

Michael had not been happy with this Earth mission and had felt a little detatched from it all as it didn't involve him.

"Michael, I know you feel your nose has been put out with all this talk about the mission on Earth, it has been the talk of the town and the young recruits have been preoccupied with it, but soon they will be on their way and then it is all about the fight going on in the Astral Planes. We need to make some sort of plan now, so we can prepare ourselves. Can I let it to you to gather all the other Archangels and Angels into the halls say for next week sometime?"

"I will do my best Merlin" Michael replied feeling slightly better now he had something to do.

"Good, keep me updated and once you have a day and time arranged let me know, and Michael, thank you" Merlin replied walking back towards the entrance of the Halls of Knowledge.

Michael turned and made his way back to the young recruits who were now waiting for him to assess them.

Mother Mary was walking to see if Merlin was in his room and met Merlin in the hallway.

"Oh Merlin, I was just coming to see you, are you going back to your place?"

"Yes Mother Mary and I'm glad you are here as we can now talk. Come in, come in, take a seat, you know I'm really concerned about Sophia, I'm not sure I can convince her, Mother Mary" Merlin said as he switched the kettle on. "I'm assuming you would like a cup of tea Mother Mary?"

"Yes please Merlin, we need to find someone who will be willing to stand by her, I feel she does need another recruit to make her feel safe enough to go and do this mission. I did see Zee talking with her earlier and also Jazz would be good, the three of them would be good for one another."

Passing Mother Mary a mug of tea, Merlin replied "Mmm I spoke to Zee earlier about Sophia, he has got a soft spot for her, I didn't expect him to go and talk with her though, I wonder how he got on? I'm not sure Zee would be good for her though, he has that fearless arrogant side to him he could lead her into a dangerous place."

"Merlin, do not underestimate Sophia, she is far more strong minded than you think. She may be brilliant for Zee!"

"Yes, yes I agree, she is strong, maybe you are right. Let's put them together along with Jazz and hope that Sophia finds the courage to do this mission."

"I'll find Jazz and let her know and pass this information on to Zee, see how he feels, about it. In the meantime maybe you can speak with Sophia again and put it to her?"

"Ok, yes I shall Mother Mary."

"Now I must go and try to catch Jazz before she begins her task and try to have a chat with the other recruits before the next meeting, tomorrow isn't it?"

"Yes, tomorrow 11am just after breakfast."

"Ok I'll catch you later, oh and Merlin, smashing cup of tea!" Mother Mary smiled and left.

Sophia was walking towards Merlin's room and passed Mother Mary in the hall and smiles.

"Are you on your way to see Merlin Sophia?"

"Yes, is he in?"

"Yes he is, I think he was hoping to speak to you."

"Oh, all good I hope?" Sophia replied.

"Yes, I must dash Sophia, I have to find Jazz, we'll speak soon ok."

"Yes, soon."

Sophia knocked on Merlin's door, it sounded too quiet on the heavy oak wood so she decided to give a harder thump and just as she did, Merlin's door swung open.

"Sophia, I heard you the first time, it just takes me a while to get to the door these days."

"Oh I'm sorry I didn't mean to, I mean I didn't think my first knock was hard enough so…."

"Yes, I know, come in, come in."

"Merlin…"

"Before you talk, could you listen to me first? I've spoken to Mother Mary about your concerns and we have spoken at length, there are also other young recruits who in confidence have come to us and asked if it is possible to be stationed near you so you can help each other and remind each other why you are on the Earth Plane. Mother Mary and I believe that this is a good idea and have decided that we should let some recruits group up and go together and that their lives will cross and be connected. By doing this we believe there will be a greater chance of there being a strong force to wake up the People of the Light and push the People of the Dark back into the balance. Mother Mary and I agree that with groups of recruits being together the chances of success will be greater than recruits going it alone. What do you think? Do you feel any better about this mission now I've explained a bit more?"

"I think it's a better idea although I still feel it's hopeless, I feel it's too big for us, I mean these Earth people have been living this way for such a long time, I feel we will be scoffed at, no one will believe us and what we are trying to do. I mean can you just imagine it Merlin, us trying to explain to the People of the Earth ~ We are here to bring the Earth back into balance and to stop the People of the Dark from taking over, by waking you, the People of the Light up! ~ It's laughable Merlin, they are not going to buy into that! Also, who is to say we won't actually say that to a Person of the Dark and they then try to stop us by putting us under attack."

"Sophia, the People of the Dark will not be drawn to you, they will stay away from you! Your light will be too bright for them, they will know who you are and they will stay away. The only people that will come to you are those People of the Light who are lost and scared and need you all to show them the way, once again. Yes, they will challenge you and may even judge you and eventually walk away, but that doesn't mean all is lost, they will either find you again or find another recruit who will help them."

"Merlin, I'm just not up to the job."

"Sophia, my dear, this is not like you at all, you are normally so positive, I just don't understand where you are coming from."

"Fear, mainly, Merlin, pure fear, all the other recruits have this excitement about them and they are wanting this mission, I wish I could feel the same, I really do, but I just have this knowing that this is going to be an impossible mission, this feeling I have in my stomach of pure hopelessness, just won't leave me."

"What is the main thing that you are fearful of Sophia?"

"Ok, you said, the People of the Dark will not be drawn to me, they will stay away from me."

"Yes, this is true."

"However, in the meeting you said we will have to be careful to not lose ourselves to the dark and get sucked in by the dark and forget our mission and who we are."

"Correct, I did say that, I'm pleased you were listening Sophia. Ok, what I mean is the People of the Dark are also on a mission, a mission to suck the People of the Light into their illusion. The People of the Dark are abusing their power and now believe that they can take over Planet Earth without having Light People to bring balance. This is happening. Our Planet Earth, like I've explained if nothing changes, our Earth will implode like it did many years ago and we will be back to nothing. You will not attract People of the Dark to you to wake them up, only the lost lights will be attracted to you. However, People of the Dark will try and suck you into their illusion. Having said that my dear Sophia, you will know who these People of the Dark are, you have a strong intuition and you listen to it, just like now, and maybe you are right in what you feel, but we cannot just sit back here and watch the Earth and the whole Universe get destroyed without helping to save it. I know I'd rather know that we did our very best to save it and we can then go with good grace, rather than knowing we allowed it to happen. After all what have we got to lose? If your feeling is a hopeless one, and if your feeling is right, we have nothing to lose, but everything to gain, even if the odds are against us, why not die trying?"

"Well there is my fear of losing myself and getting sucked into that illusion. You say I will know who these people are and I have strong intuition but that's here not there, I suppose it comes down to not trusting myself, there I said it out loud, I'm scared because I don't trust myself. I fear betraying myself and others and getting sucked into the dark, because I want the easy option. I don't like confrontation, I don't want to not be liked. I'm scared of standing up for my beliefs or just standing up for myself and there in that place, it will be just like last time, I lost who I was Merlin, I lied and cheated to save myself. I don't want to go back there, I love it here, I can be me and remain true to myself and everybody knows me, me the real me, my faults, my love, me, everything I believe in here, I'm at home here, everyone is the same here and we are learning all the time, about being a better Person of Light, a more unconditional person. I am so sorry Merlin, I just can't help how I feel." Sophia sighed.

Merlin stayed quiet for a minute, before he spoke, more gently, more softly.

"Sophia you have nothing to apologise for, what you have just said, was exactly how I felt many, many years ago when I too, did not trust myself one bit, I too betrayed myself to save myself. I totally understand where you are at. Can I ask you Sophia, how long have you been here with us?"

"Erm, I came to you about fifteen years ago."

"And why or what was it that made you choose this place?"

"For sanctuary, Merlin and a break, I didn't want to incarnate any more I wanted to just find me again. I wanted peace, I wanted to just be, no pretending, no more trying to fit in, no more trying to please everyone."

"Ok and you now feel you have peace and you are happy where you are?"

"Yes I'm very happy, I know me, I've learned so much here about myself and about others, I enjoy my lessons and my tasks. I'm finally comfortable with who I am."

"So what, out of everything you have learnt would you say has been your greatest lesson so far?"

"Mmm that's a tough question erm… I believe my greatest lesson is to always remain true to yourself, regardless of what others think of you, although I have also come to realise that here, I'm liked far more than I thought and just by remaining myself, other recruits really like me, which I find quite overwhelming."

"So you are happy with what you found, once you uncovered the real you, you have found yourself and you are now very comfortable with you, I get it and totally understand what you are saying Sophia as I too have lived the lives similar to yourself and I too am happy with me. However, on Earth there are People of the Light that are also living the lives that you once lived. These lost lights are crying out for someone to help them find their self worth and self love, and as this starts to happen, the Earth will start to come into balance. It is our time to intervene Sophia and time for you to now put into practice all that you have learnt. Sometimes you are called to practise what you have learnt outside your comfort zone, in other words feel the fear and do it anyway. Believe me Sophia, I would not be asking you all to do this mission if I didn't think it was necessary. I too will be working, alongside the Gods and Archangels on the different Astral Planes to help bring the Universe back into balance. You see it's not just Mother Earth that needs help, it's the whole Universe".

"I understand what you are saying Merlin, I just still don't trust myself enough."

"Well my dear Sophia, there is still time, I cannot force you to do anything."

"I know, I think I'm just going to leave decision making for now and see how I feel after the next meeting."

"Oh yes, the meeting tomorrow, I have to go and prepare, I'm sure I will have lots of questions to answer!"

"Merlin, before you go, can I ask what was your life like before you ended up here, helping others?"

"Oh Sophia, it's a long story and it's not just this life, it's many others too."

"Please Merlin, you said my thoughts and feelings and life are similar to yours and your life, I'm curious to know how you managed to turn it all around and to be who you are today."

"Well you'd better sit back down then, and make sure you are comfy, this may take a while".

Chapter Four
Merlin's Journey

"Where to begin…"

"My life has many twists and turns and many people have different stories about me, most of them are true, so I will begin not at the beginning but at the end of where I was before I found myself here."

"I escaped society, people and their laws and rules and controlling behaviours by living deep in the forest. You see like you I betrayed myself to fit in with others and I was used for my knowledge and my 'magic', but this soon turned into being bullied into doing spells and tricks to harm others and I knew it was wrong, but I felt totally trapped. It was easier and safer to become like them than it was to stand up for my beliefs and stand alone."

"One day I had done something really awful that I struggle to forgive myself for and don't even want to talk about even now. Not feeling good about myself late one night I vowed to get away, even if it meant leaving behind the ones that were needing my help I needed to live my truth and if that meant being forever on my own so be it."

"So in the early hours of the morning I left what I called home and headed into the forest."

"I decided to be alone and reconnect with myself, not just my body, but all of me, I had been too long with others, I had lost my way and become like them. My soul needed me to return and it was glad when I did. Removing the cloak I had been so comfortable with for so long was hard. This cloak was who I thought I was, who I had become over the years, little did I know that it was what others had made me. Removing something that has 'served' you for so long is a scary process as I had no idea of who I would find once my protection, my cloak had gone, but escaping from the world and being on my own with just myself, I began to rediscover who I was."

"It took me 10 whole days to get deep enough into the forest to feel secure enough to never be found and safe enough to have a fire that no one would be able to see the smoke. Those 10 whole days were a journey in themselves, I mean could you be a day on your own with no distractions and only your mind to keep you company? I mean most people wouldn't last an hour let alone a day, and yet walking and resting for 10 days with no change of scenery or seeing another soul some days I would believe I was going crazy because I would think I had seen someone and speed up and shout out 'hey', but there wasn't anybody there, just my mind creating something that wasn't there."

"Merlin, can I just stop you there and ask a question?"

"Ah, Sophia, you are going to ask me why I didn't use my 'magic' to transport me into the place I needed to be aren't you?"

"Wow, yes I was just curious to know if you have the magic gift, how come you didn't use it?"

"Forever curious, never change that trait about yourself Sophia, wherever you end up, always, always ask questions! Sometimes Sophia it's good to not have the magic at the end of my fingertips, it's better to find the magic in the experience. I had made a vow not to use the magic I had because I had abused it for the bad and not the good; I decided to get where I needed to be with just myself, no magic, I needed to embrace this journey, go back to who I was without my gifts of magic and wisdom, I needed to just be."

"Ah ok, that makes sense, please Merlin continue."

"Well, I found myself deep enough in the forest to make a home for myself, so I started to look for wood to create a shelter…"

"Without using your magic?"

"Yes Sophia no magic involved, like I said I wanted to experience life without magic. So, 6 days later my shelter was built and I looked at it with pride knowing that I had achieved something all by myself. Now don't get me wrong, it wasn't perfect, but it did a good job keeping me dry and warm and out of the way of danger. I slept so well once I finished it." Merlin chuckled to himself as he remembered.

"The feeling the next morning as I woke up felt just like magic. I was taken in by the beauty of this amazing place, the stillness, the colours and sounds, so far removed from where I had come from and, for the first time in a long time, I felt good. The journey to get there was a hard one, I lived with a fear that someone would find me and take me back. I had a fear I was being hunted by people who wanted me back, but only for their personal gain. When I became tired and weary I would have to stop and rest, but this again was not complete rest as I had to have my wits about me the whole time, listening to every sound and being aware of every movement that caught my eye."

"During those 10 days I learnt a lot about myself. I learned that I was stronger than I thought I was not just physically, but mentally I was strong too. I also learnt that I actually enjoyed my own company and the silence. For those 10 days I remembered who I really was and was shocked at myself as I realised how much of myself I had lost to just fit in with everyone else. That moment really made me sad. I had betrayed myself for the sake of others. At that moment I realised that I had done this for many lifetimes and I made a vow to myself that this would be the last time. Never again would I live a lie, no matter what."

"Merlin, it's ok if you would rather not talk about it, but what happened before you made your escape, where were you and who were you with?"

"It's not that I don't want to talk about it, it just doesn't feel like it was me now, after all this time I have remained true to myself so going back there seems so strange for me. Also we haven't got time right now for me to tell you the story of my life, we need to get back to the present day and the mission on the Earth Plane."

"Now I've got to go and get prepared, so i will see you tomorrow after breakfast"

"Ok Merlin, Thank you for talking to me"

Merlin smiled and followed her out of his room.

Chapter Five
Nerves

It was morning and Sophia stretched and yawned, still sleepy her morning had come round far too quickly for her liking.

She had struggled to get to sleep last night and kept waking up from restless sleep throughout the night. She took another look at the time, it was 07.13 am, exactly 13 minutes since the alarm woke her, was this an omen that today would not go as planned? Putting her pillow back over her face to block out the sun streaming through her window in the vain hope she would drift back off to sleep for 5 more minutes, but it was hopeless.

Sophia sat up, still sleepy, but allowing her feet to hit the ground. She stood up and walked over to the window. Outside there were a few recruits walking about, the gardens were looking so beautiful once again as all the flowers were starting to bloom and show off their stunning colours and beauty. She turned from the window and began to think about getting dressed.

Meanwhile, the Hall was full of excited, energetic young recruits queuing up for their breakfast. Their loud chatter was made louder by the high ceilings of the Hall. Zee sat himself down and started tucking into his big breakfast.

"Wow, have you actually got an appetite Zee?" Nathalie asked as she sat down next to him with just a cup of coffee.

"Yes, of course, nothing would change my appetite Nathalie!" he replied with a wink.

"Well fair play to your stomach, mine is in knots this morning!"

"Ah you're worrying unnecessarily, we have it all sorted, it's going to be ok."

"I wish I had your confidence Zee!" Nathalie laughed nervously.

"Hey, Zee, Nathalie have any of you seen Sophia this morning?" Jazz asked as she walked over to their table.

"No, not yet, but it is early, maybe she is still sorting her head out." Zee replied.

"Mmm, maybe."

"Huh, unlike you Zee who has food on your mind from the minute you wake up. I can't blame her if she is still in her room. If she feels anything like me, I couldn't face breakfast either." Nathalie chuckled.

"Oh me too!" said Jazz, "even the thought of food has me feeling sick, my stomach is full of butterflies this morning, I can't even think straight."

"The trouble with you girls is you are lightweights, you need to become a bit more hardcore like us boys." Zee said, stuffing another piece of bacon into his mouth,

"Sometimes Zee you are just so arrogant and big headed!"

"Hey, I'm only joking, don't take me too seriously it's my sense of humour, really I know you girls are nervous, and yes the nerves have kicked in for me as well, but I decided to eat lots to get these nerves in order. Come on, I'm sorry."

"Zee, you just need to hear yourself sometimes. Your humour is not funny!" said Jazz as she turned and walked away.

"Well now I've finished my coffee I'm out of here too, enjoy your breakfast Zee" said Nathalie.

"Yes I will, see you soon Nat."

Sophia could smell the cooked breakfast as she made her way to the Hall, but she was unsure whether she could actually stomach any food whatsoever. Although she knew that if she didn't eat the empty feeling that she

felt inside would steal her energy and she definitely needed some energy right now.

The Hall was less busy now and as Sophia walked in she noticed Zee just finishing his breakfast, but deep in conversation with Lee, Jason and two other recruits she didn't know. He was laughing with them and appeared to be so relaxed. She walked over to the food and decided on a bacon roll with a cup of tea and hoped that that would keep her going until lunch.

Zee spotted her from across the Hall and called her over.

"Hey Soph, come and sit with us!"

Sophia found herself blushing slightly, but tried to act normally. As she walked over she thought to herself that she needed to sort this out, he was only being friendly, nothing had changed for him. Hopefully, he hadn't noticed her red cheeks, she needed to get herself back under control.

"Hey, are you good?" Sophia asked as she sat down.

"Yes, I'm good, we are all good aren't we lads?"

"Yep, sure!" replied Lee and Jason.

"We were just talking about the meeting really and what's going to happen next."

"Mmm, can't say I've made my mind up yet to be honest with you, my stomach is churning, but I'm eating because if I don't eat my energy goes. It's a bit like chewing cardboard at the minute though, I'm telling you!" Sophia laughed, trying her best to not blush again.

"Right, that's me finished. I'm just going for a walk around the gardens to see if I can find Jay. Are you coming Zee, Lee?" said Jason.

"No, you go, I'll catch you out there in a bit." said Zee.

"Yep, I'm coming!" Lee said, standing up and finishing his tea. "See you later then Zee."

"Yep, see you soon!" Zee replied.

"Bye guys!"

"Bye Soph!" Lee and Jason said in unison.

"So you're still undecided then Soph?" said Zee.

"Yes, still not sure, I just really don't know what to do, I suppose it's fear mainly as well as the unknown, jumping out of my comfort zone!"

"But we are all doing that Soph, we will all be there together so we won't actually be doing it on our own will we?"

"Yes but will we actually remember that fact Zee will we remember who we are and why we are actually there? I mean it's easy to 'know' that while we are still here, but once we incarnate will we remember that we are on a mission?"

"Soph, do you think that Merlin would send us on a mission that he felt was impossible?"

"How can you be so sure?" Sophia sighed.

Zee smiled. "Because Merlin knows we can achieve this, he has faith and he believes in us. If he thought for one minute that we were too naïve and novices, he would have to consider asking the Archangels and the Older Angels, whereas he has asked us and the Older Angels and Archangels have the task of a much tougher mission. Plus I'm a great believer in 'everything is impossible until someone makes it possible'." Zee looked straight into Sophia's eyes and smiled. "You can do this Soph, I'll have your back."

Sophia shook her head. "That's only if you remember me and who you are, and if we are in the same area!"

"Ye have little faith!" Zee replied pushing back his chair and standing up. "I've got to go and catch up with the lads, but I'll see you later, yes?"

"Yes, of course you will, see you soon."

Sophia followed him with her eyes as he walked towards the door and then caught herself smiling, blushing again. She quickly finished her tea and headed back to her room.

Once she got there Sophia decided to make a list of 'For' and 'Against' as she still had no clue what decision to make. Sitting at her dressing table with pen in hand, ready to write, she caught sight of herself in the mirror. She looked at her reflection, staring back at her was someone she was familiar with, but she didn't know, not truly know.

Sophia spoke out loud, "Who are you?" Finding herself being pulled in by her own brown eyes, she quickly pulled away knowing that she was not ready to see herself. To distract herself she began to write her list:

FOR	AGAINST
Help people/service to others	*Judgement*
Be with friends	*Betrayal*
Teach others	*Lose myself*
Give love/hope	*Lose others*

A knock on her door broke her concentration, she stopped writing to go and see who it was.

"Hi, I'm not disturbing you am I?" Jazz said as she opened the door.

"No, I'm only writing a list to see if I can make a decision."

"Really? You still haven't decided?"

"Nope, have you?"

"Yes, I'm going to give it a try, I'm a little apprehensive, but I'm going to do my best. Although, I would be happier if you were coming with me."

Sophia sighed. "I know you would, but I'm still so unsure and I don't want to make the wrong choice so I'm just sitting with it for a little longer in the hope that these nerves die down as they are not helping me at all!"

"Tell me about it! Now I've made the decision to go, these nerves are stopping me from eating!" Jazz laughed.

Sophia smiled. "Come on, let's get out of here for a bit, let's go for a walk."

Sophia slipped on her shoes and they both set off out of her room.

Chapter Six
Persistance

Merlin found Zee walking with Lee, and called out to him. Zee turned round and saw Merlin.

"Hey lads, I'll catch up with you in a bit, Merlin wants to see me."

"OK Zee, usual place, under the cherry tree?" Lee said.

"Yep, see you in a bit". Zee replied and started to walk towards Merlin. "Hey Merlin what's up?"

"Er the sky" Merlin replied with a smile.

"Eh?"

"It was a joke Zee, you said what's up, I replied the sky!" Merlin rolled his eyes "Never mind Zee, I'm sorry for pulling you away from your friends."

"That's ok Merlin, what's…oh I get it ha ha, what's the problem?"

"No problem at all, I just wanted to talk with you for a bit, Mother Mary has had a visit from Jazz, and she told Mother Mary that Sophia was undecided still, and would it be at all possible if they could be somehow be put near each other so they could find each other, and then help each other with the mission too". Zee could feel himself blushing, Merlin must have noticed too, because he held Zee's arm and said "Come on let's walk."

They walked in silence, until they got to the Contemplation Gardens and sat on a bench, surrounded by the high hedges and trees. After a while Zee spoke.

"I believe Sophia will be good on this mission, Merlin, and between you and I, I have got a bit of a soft spot for her. She seems so vulnerable at times, but also so strong, I would love to cross paths with her on Earth and work together on this mission, but she can't make her mind up, and time is getting on."

"Mmm yes I know, I will try to find her again and speak to her once more." Merlin said. "And you know Zee, you are right in what you say, she will be good on Earth". "She will, I know she will and also if our paths cross I know she will be good for me, and Jazz of course."

"Well Mother Mary and I have spoken to the Council of Five to see if it could be possible for your paths to cross, this has been agreed, but you all are not to meet at once, and you will only get one shot at meeting, possible at a push two, so you must keep aware, when you are on Earth at all times, which will be difficult, if you have forgotten that you are on a mission, once you are there, but fingers crossed that will not happen, and that is if Sophia decides to go with you."

"Well that's good, if Sophia does indeed change her mind, however, if she chooses to stay, there isn't much we can do is there?"

"Sophia, like you, has free will, we cannot force her to do anything she doesn't want to Zee, so no we cannot do much, but I will find her and have a last attempt at persuading her to go."

"and even if Sophia does choose not to go, you, Jazz and the others will be just fine and you will do just as good without Sophia, trust me".

"I know Merlin, it's just, I would feel much better if Sophia was with us, just knowing she was somewhere on Earth, would be enough, I believe Jazz feels the same too". "Oh I know Jazz feels the same Zee, she has expressed her concerns with Mother Mary, which is why we had a meeting with the council of five and we have agreed that at some point in your time on Earth, your paths will cross. So hopefully Sophia will choose to do this mission".

"We can only hope Merlin."

"Does Jazz know that there is a possibility of our paths crossing?"

"I believe Mother Mary has told Jazz Zee, and that reminds me we have another meeting soon, we all have to meet at the Halls of Knowledge, so I'm going to have to get myself over there, and you best come too". Merlin stood up and Zee followed him out of the Gardens.

Jazz had left Sophia in her room and decided she would try and find Zee and let him know what Mother Mary had told her, about them all being together on Earth. As she walked through the corridors, she caught sight of him just coming in from the gardens with Merlin.

"Zee!" she called out to him waving. Zee turned and saw it was Jazz.

"Er Merlin, I'll meet you there, Jazz is calling me."

"Ok Zee." Merlin said not even stopping, just lifting his arm and waving.

"Hey Jazz, what's up?" Zee smiled to himself realising that he had said what's up quite a few times lately.

"Hey!" Jazz replied just catching her breath, that little jog to get to Zee had got her out of breath.

"Are you ok?" Zee chuckled.

"Yes never better." Jazz replied puffing her cheeks out. "I believe I need more exercise, I'm starting to get unfit! Anyway I called out to you, as I managed to speak to Mother Mary about whether…"

Jazz looked at Zee as Zee put his hand up with a smile. "What?"

"I know Jazz, Merlin has just spoken to me and told me."

"He did?"

"Yep, and it sounds great, now all we have to do is convince Soph."

"That will be easier said than done."

"Ah you too eh, she is really stubborn, she won't budge, not even a teeny bit. Tell me about it Zee, I have begged, and pleaded with her, she won't make a decision."

"Nope, I know, I will try again, but as Merlin says, she has free will and we cannot force her to do anything".

"No we sure can't force her, anyway I need to get myself over to the Great Halls of Knowledge for the next meeting. Maybe we will find Sophia there and we can both talk to her."

"Yes me too, although I need to find Abe, I need to tell him something, and Merlin said he would try and talk with Sophia, so maybe leave Sophia to Merlin for a while, he may have a better chance of convincing her this mission is a good idea".

"Ok Zee, well I hope he can, time is running out and we cannot miss our departure."

"I know Jazz, I'll catch up with you soon."

"Ok, I'll see you in a bit." Zee walked back out into the Gardens to see if Abe was out there and Jazz made her way to the Halls of Knowledge.

Chapter Seven
The Fear

Staring at a card that had fallen out of the writing pad, Sophia let out the breath she had been holding. She had been busy, sorting out her room and trying to organise her paperwork into some orderly fashion, and that is when a card fell onto the floor from her writing pad. Talking to herself, she bent down picked it up, "Oh why did you have to appear again." Looking at it more closely in her hand, she already knew the answer to the question. It was giving her another sign. "What to do?" she said quietly. It was an Oracle card, and now it was staring up at her, this beautiful picture of a young blonde haired girl with a ball of light coming out of her hands, the message above her head *'You are a powerful lightworker'* and underneath in small writing *'It is safe for you to be powerful, your spiritual power brings great blessings in loving service to the Divine'*. She knew she had this card as she had been given it, in one of her classes, and yet, she had forgotten all about it and now here it was, looking up at her with the message once again, stinging her eyes.

The time had come for Merlin to call everyone back to the Great Halls of knowledge, and Sophia still was not convinced this was a good idea. The whole place was buzzing with similar conversations, and everyone was excited. As Sophia made her way to the Great Halls of Knowledge, she saw that Zee was up ahead, laughing and joking with two of his friends. How can he be so calm and relaxed about this mission, she wondered, staring down the corridor at him. She studied his face, his eyes actually smiled, when he did, he was tall, with broad shoulders and he was in proportion, his legs not too short, his body not too long. He clearly had a sense of humour, as his two friends were laughing hysterically at whatever it was he was saying. Just for a second he glanced back and met Sophia's eyes, but looked back at his friends and started again to make them laugh. It was as if the look he gave her was enough to say "I see you."

Sophia found herself blushing and purposely slowing down, to allow others to pass her, but more for Zee to go ahead, she really didn't need him to see her flushed cheeks.

"Boo!" Jazz screamed as she grabbed Sophia's shoulders.

Sophia turned around and said "Oh it's you!"

"How comes you never jump? The amount of times I try and get a reaction out of you, it's impossible, it's as if you always know I'm there!" said Jazz as she rolled her eyes.

"Well I do know you are there, I can feel your energy Jazz, duh." Sophia laughed.

"Well can you feel everyone's energy, cos I know others that have tried to spook you and you just don't get spooked."

"Well let's just say I'm ready for *almost anything*."

"That you are indeed! Anyway are you going to do this mission or not?"

Sophia looked sideways at Jazz, she knew Jazz was looking straight at her, Sophia took a deep breath in and let it out slowly. Jazz didn't take her eyes off Sophia.

Sophia feeling the pressure of Jazz's stare, slowed her walking down even more. Jazz still said nothing, but matched Sophia's pace.

"Oh Jazz, you actually want me to answer a question I don't even know the answer to myself!"

"Really, you still don't know? Jeez what is stopping you from making a decision?"

"Do you really want to know?" Sophia asked.

"Duh, yes!" Jazz said throwing her hands up in the air. "You, well not just you, there are others too, but you…"

"Me!" Jazz exclaimed. "Why me?" I wouldn't want you to make the decision because of me!"

Sophia tried to stay calm so she could explain. "No, I know that silly, but you are my friend here and I have a few others I truly love with all my heart and because of that I would make the decision to come to Earth as I wouldn't want to lose any of you. However, the thought of going fills me with dread, because personally I feel it's a hopeless mission and I'm so scared that not only will I lose you, but if I come with you, I will lose myself also. Jazz I don't want to lose me, or forget who I am, or why I'm there, you know, forget we ever had a purpose? Just get sucked in like everyone else."

"Wow!" said Jazz now walking, looking down at the floor.

"Yep, wow, so no I can't make a decision, I'm torn, I'm scared and I don't want to fail." Sophia paused, surprised she actually said that out loud. "There I said it, I don't want to fail."

Suddenly Sophia had realised her real fear, it was failure, normally she was good at failing, it never stopped her trying, in all of her tasks, if she failed, she would try and try again. This time was different though, if she failed, she knew, there would be no time to try again, it would be game over. This was a mission and succeeding was the only option. This was where she really had to believe in herself and there was no room for failure. She had to believe in herself, that she could do this mission and make a difference. "Wow!" Sophia thought to herself, I didn't see that coming, fear of failure, wow."

Jazz had now stopped walking, but was deep in thought, still looking at the floor. "Jazz, are you ok?" Sophia asked.

"Yeah, I think, I mean that was heavy stuff that you said back there, I mean woah, you've made me think, that's for sure!"

"Mmm I know, but that's what I'm struggling with, which is why I still can't decide." "Sophia, I believe in you, I believe you can make a difference, I believe you can succeed, I believe you can do this, you have got this, but you are right, you have to believe in you. Listen, I have to go find my friend Sara, but I'll catch up with you soon, ok? I'll meet you in the

Great Halls of Knowledge". She hugged Sophia and turned and walked in the direction of where Zee was walking.

Sophia's first thought was, I hope she doesn't bump into Zee and tell him what we spoke about, that would be the last thing I need. Sophia shrugged her shoulders as if to shrug off the heaviness of deciding and walked towards Merlin's room, hoping he would be there.

Knocking on Merlin's door, Sophia quietly prayed he would be there. There was the sound a click of a lock, the latch lifting and the door opening. Merlin was standing on a ladder inside.

"Come in Sophia, don't stand there waiting for an invite, come in!"

Sophia walked in and closed the door behind her. Merlin appeared to be looking for something on the tall book case.

"Have you lost something Merlin?" Sophia asked.

"Er yes my wand, well erm not my usual wand, but the one that, oh never mind, I'll find it soon enough, anyway". Merlin carried on whilst climbing down the stair ladder. "To what do I owe this pleasure?" As he reached the last step he looked over at her,

"I'm just really scared Merlin and just can't make a decision.

"I'm sensing your fear Sophia, what is it you fear so badly, it stops you from moving forward?"

Sophia looked straight into Merlin's eyes, here it is again, that same feeling, and now she was being asked to say it out loud again. Sophia could feel herself, getting hot, her heart beating so loudly that she could hear it in her ears. She took a deep breath in and then spoke. "I am scared of failing Merlin" tears pricked her eyes, why is this bothering me so much she thought.

Merlin's whole face and eyes softened. "My dear Sophia, failure is only made true, when you don't try."

"Have you ever failed at anything Merlin?" Sophia asked quietly.

"I've never seen it as failure, my dear Sophia, I have only ever seen it as not succeeding in my goal, but then there is always something to learn in not succeeding. A lesson is always present, if only we were to see it."

Merlin smiled softly at her and started to tell her a story about a little boy who was walking along the beach, and saw hundreds of starfish washed up along the shore, he ran towards them bending down picking up as many as he could and throw them back into the sea, he had been doing this for quite a while, when a man who had been watching from a distance, walked over to the boy and said "Boy, why are you bothering, can't you see, your task is impossible, there are hundreds here, you are never going to make a difference!" The little boy stopped for a second and looked up at the man, still holding a starfish and then threw it into the sea, he then turned back to the man and said "I made a difference to that one."

There was a silence and Sophia realised she had silent tears falling onto her cheeks. "That was beautiful." she whispered.

"And not once did you think that little boy had failed, Sophia, I have to say neither did that boy, he never felt a failure, because he didn't manage to save them all, he knew he had done his best and he knew he made a difference."

Sophia sat down, in Merlin's big high backed armchair, surprisingly it was not as hard as it looked and suddenly she felt very comfortable and small, a bit like Alice in Wonderland when she shrunk to get through the tiny door.

Shaking her head, she replied "No he had not failed at all, he at least tried to do something."

"Yes Sophia, he had tried and he learnt that in his attempt to save them, he made a big difference to the ones he did save unlike the man, the boy found courage to try. You see Sophia, you have to change the way you think. Sometimes when you do something that is not in alignment with your soul, you have to listen to it, if you don't pay attention to that inner voice or gut instinct and continue anyway regardless, eventually after many blocks, distractions and obstacles, which may I add are your souls way of saying stop, don't do it, wrong way, don't go there, you still go ahead regardless, and then at the end, you feel as if you have failed. In fact you were not meant to be doing it in the first place, you were on the wrong path and not in alignment with your soul. But you can't see it that way you just see failure and then tell yourself 'I'm not good enough'. This happens in every area of your life and not just your life, but everyone's life. It's safe here, I agree, and here you are in alignment with your soul, but only because of what you have learnt."

---

* Starfish story adapted from the original by Loren Eiseley. Life's a dance.

"Sometimes others will, as you say fail, but they try again and do something different and succeed, it has still been incredibly hard, but they achieved their goal, this time, and that's because they had to learn something about themselves or the subject before they could get into alignment with their soul. Let me tell you a little secret Sophia about the young recruits who will step forward and go on this mission. The young recruits that sign up for this mission are listening to their inner voice and following their gut feeling, they are in alignment with their soul. There are other young recruits that will be signing up for this mission but their inner voice and gut feeling is telling them not to. They are not in alignment with their soul, but do you know they will sign up anyway, they will ignore their inner voice and gut feeling, they will ignore their own truth, because they don't want to be judged or seen as a failure and they want to be like the others. These young recruits will most probably be the ones that get lost or will get called home, because they have not lived their own truth or listened to their inner voice and they are not in alignment with their soul. Then there are other young recruits that will not sign up, and they will listen to their gut feeling and inner voice telling them, this is not the right time. They will be staying behind and by making the right decision and living their truth, they become in alignment with their soul. These young recruits will be just as important staying here helping those that go and do this mission. No one fails."

"Getting back to your question, have I ever failed? I've only ever seen it as not succeeding in my goal. When I was a lot younger, a lot younger," Merlin looked over the top of his spectacles, straight into Sophia's eyes, "I was sure my purpose was to create magic, be creative and create spells and potions and yes, I did that for a while, but when I didn't succeed, when I no longer was achieving the effects I wanted to achieve, I had to admit I no longer loved my 'purpose', I began to hate every bit of it. I lost my passion for magic. I was really sad about it, because without the magic, who was Merlin? I defined myself by the magic I made, but that was not who I was, so I began my own journey of 'self' discovery. Oh boy, was that a journey." Merlin chuckled, staring into thin air as if he was reliving it all over again.

"Merlin." Sophia said bringing Merlin back into the room.

"What, oh er yes, sorry, went off course for a bit, right where was I?"

Sophia giggled, Merlin did make her laugh sometimes. "You were saying you lost your passion for magic and went on a journey to discover who you were" Sophia reminded him.

"Oh yes, that was it, well the rest is history as they say, because I actually learnt that my passion was helping and serving others, helping others find themselves and discover who they really were and help them find their true purpose. In the early days when my magic was my passion, it was in preparation for my life now. My magic was not my life purpose though and it had to come to an end. However the tools and knowledge I learnt back then I have brought with me and still use to this day."

"Merlin, what is my purpose?" Sophia asked.

"Sophia I believe you already know, your purpose, but you are resisting it, because you do not want to fail, my dear Sophia, your job is not to be responsible all by yourself for this mission. Your job is not to save the Earth, your job is far more important than that. Your job is to go and shine your light on everyone you meet, so they too, will begin to shine brightly again and eventually the few lights that you have made a difference to will also make a difference to others and soon lots more lights will start to shine brightly and your light and their light will create a ripple effect that will spread far and wide and eventually together, you will shine as one and the Earth will come into balance once more."

"Look at it this way, on your own, you see this mission as an impossible one, now close your eyes and visualize a million trillion lights, just like fire flies – the light, and yet it is a million single lights, making a difference and you are a part of it. That , my dear Sophia is your purpose. The question is will you live it?"

Merlin turned to look at Sophia as loud knock on the door disturbed them both. "Come in, come in!" Merlin shouted walking his way towards the door.

"I'm not disturbing anything am I?" Archangel Michael said as he peered around the door.

"No, not at all, Michael, in fact I was just leaving. Thank you Merlin, I needed this chat, but I do have some work still to do, so I will leave you two alone." She leaned in and gave Merlin a little kiss on his cheek.

"Yes ok Sophia, we will talk again soon", Merlin replied.

Sophia closed the door behind her, and walked back towards her room.

Chapter Eight
The dark

"Well Michael, I haven't seen you since the meeting, you haven't been sulking have you?" Merlin asked with a twinkle in his eye.

"Actually, no not sulking," Archangel Michael replied "I've been researching after what you said about us having our own fight in the Universe, I thought that I had better get some knowledge of the war that is going on out there."

"Ah very good Michael, I hope you kept discreet, we don't want to cause a drama unnecessarily do we?"

"They didn't even know I was there." said Michael with a smile.

"So are you happy with your research?"

"Well I found that you, Merlin, were right, it's a mess out there, I mean chaos, a lot of fighting and imbalance, it is not calm and serene! To be fair Merlin I was shocked, I've never seen it so bad."

"Mmm," Merlin replied once again deep in thought, "the thing is Michael, we cannot go in there, fighting, we will just add to the chaos and imbalance, because they will believe we are just coming to take over, and take their power away, but it's knowing how to 'get in' and let them know we are not there to attack but to try and help." "Merlin, they didn't even know I was there!" Archangel Michael chuckled. "They are so busy fighting, and shouting at each other, they didn't even notice I was out there. You should see Zeus and Thor fighting for power, and then Helios deciding he would like a part of it and yet everyone is so blind to the dark forces, that are now so close and of course, they are loving all this imbalance and negativity, they are feeding off of it and I can tell you Merlin, it didn't feel very nice out there at all. I really don't know how we are going to succeed in our own mission."

"Michael, that's not like you to be so negative, I told you we had a bigger battle ahead, now we have to find a way."

"I know Merlin, but I've been out there now and it's not good."

"Well we have to think Michael, really think. I may have to ask you to go back out there and just find out where are the dark forces are placed and how far in have they got? If it's over half already, we will have to act sooner than I thought, but if they are just a little way in, it may give us a bit more thinking time. We have to be smart, Michael, and think smart".

"Merlin, I don't like it out there...."

"Michael, they didn't notice you were there, your words, not mine, so now I'm asking you to please go and bring me back the information I need. My dear Michael, I thought you would be chomping at the bit to go and do something, what's happened to you?"

"I've told you Merlin, it's bigger than you think out there..."

"Er which is why we need all those Gods to stop fighting each other and pull together for once in this time!" Merlin let out a big sigh "Now go, come back with the information, I need to talk to Mother Mary."

"Ok Merlin, I will do my best."

"You always do Michael, you always do." said Merlin as he opened the door to let Michael leave.

Merlin decided it was best to go and see Mother Mary immediately, as from what Michael had said, it was not looking good. As he left his room he saw that Abe was walking past.

"Ah Abe, are you on your way to the next meeting?"

"Er yes Merlin, you did say we all had to be there didn't you?"

"Yes, yes I did, but I'm going to be about an hour late, could you let everyone know that, I must discuss the situation with Mother Mary, so our meeting will be delayed by an hour?"

Abe started to go red and flushed "Yes Merlin of course I can" Abe replied.

"Abe are you ok, you seem quite flushed?"

"I'm fine Merlin honestly." Abe was absolutely petrified, he didn't do public speaking, he had never had to speak in front of people before, but Merlin had asked him and he was not going to let Merlin down. Abe already felt that he had let everyone down by deciding not to go on the mission. He had this gut feeling telling him it was not the right time for him. So as much as he was listening to his feeling and acting on it, he felt that his friends were disappointed in him. Merlin had told him there was still a job here for him to do with other young recruits and that made him feel slightly better.

Abe entered the Great Hall of Knowledge repeating to himself in his mind, this is your moment, hold it together, you only have two sentences, it's not a lesson, it's just a message to pass on. He found that talking to himself in his head took his attention away from all those recruits!!

This was it, Abe stood up on the small platform and spoke. "Ok guys" to his surprise his voice was loud and clear. "Can you all just listen to me for a second and can you hear me right at the back?"

A resounding "YES" came straight back at him and then silence. Abe could feel himself going red, he caught himself looking down at the floor. "Speak!" he told himself and "look up". Abe looked up and said "Er Merlin is still in a meeting with Mother Mary and will be an hour late, he just wanted me to pass the message on".

A groan from the young recruits and a few thank you Abe's, and the recruits started to leave the Halls of Knowledge. Abe jumped off the platform, feeling relieved and strangely pleased he had managed to do something for Merlin. Abe found a bench and decided to wait for Merlin to arrive.

Mother Mary opened her door for Merlin. "After you Merlin".

Merlin stepped inside saying "Ah the lovely smell of Jasmine."

Mother Mary smiled at him. "It's my favourite fragrance Merlin, brings me a little peace and joy."

"Mmm whenever I smell it, Mother Mary it reminds me of you."

"Can I get you a tea, Merlin, or there is anything else you would like?"

"Tea would be fine thank you." Merlin replied walking over to the sofa.

"Here you go then, and it's ok to sit on the sofa Merlin, you don't have to stand here." Mother Mary sat down and patted the cushion beside her "Let's talk, what's so urgent?"

"Well I spoke with Archangel Michael earlier and he tells me, he has been 'researching' the battle on the Astral Planes. He says it's quite shocking out there and he even sounded a bit despairing of the mission."

"Mmm we may have to act sooner Merlin, if this is the case!" Mother Mary said.

"Well that's what I said to Michael, so I've sent him back out there, just to find out, how far the Dark have got and whether we have to act now or not."

"Good, yes excellent, when is he due back?"

"Soon I hope." Merlin replied.

"Ok have you had your meeting with the young recruits yet? Do you know how many are going to do the mission?"

"No Mother Mary, not yet I thought I would speak with you first about the chaos in the Astral Planes, but I'm going to meet with them all, in a while, well after we finish here, so do we have a plan Mother Mary?"

"Well I think we need to send the young recruits on their way and wait for them to be settled, we will need to keep a close eye on them for a while Merlin, just in case we need to abort the mission."

"I'm not sure we can abort the mission Mother Mary, if we decide to do that, then we will almost definitely have a catastrophe on our hands and we have no plan for that whatsoever."

Mother Mary smiled, she knew Merlin was right in what he was saying, there was no way they could abort the mission, this mission had to be successful. "Ok Merlin, we need to stay focused and positive! Go do the meeting, send the young recruits off on their mission, make sure they are prepared for whatever comes their way and make sure they are given all the information, and that they understand it, before they agree. Once they are on their way, we can have a meeting with all the Archangels and Senior Angels about the mission on the Astral Planes. Come and see me for our final meeting before we call the others though, Merlin, we need to be sure of the mission ourselves before we can ask the others, and we can only do that once Archangel Michael comes back with the information."

"Indeed Mother Mary, I will wait for Archangel Michael to return and we will come to you and discuss our options. Now if you will excuse me I have to go and see our young recruits."

"Ah yes of course Merlin, which reminds me, has Sophia made her decision yet?" "No not yet, I have a strange feeling, she won't go Mother Mary. I was speaking to her earlier, she was still torn and her fear of failure is blocking her way. She is putting herself under a lot of pressure and is feeling responsible for all of her friends and even making sure that we all succeed in this mission. I have told her this is not her job to take the mission on all by herself, it is her job to help others, and by helping others find their light, we will succeed. I hope she does decide to go, she will be so good at helping others and I doubt she will lose herself, I am trying hard to convince her though!"

"You know Merlin, it sounds like history repeating itself" said Mother Mary standing up, Merlin stood up to join her. She rubbed his shoulder as they walked towards the door. "Just in different forms" she continued.

Merlin smiled, he knew what she meant as it was Mother Mary who had the hard job of convincing Merlin himself, that he indeed was good at his job and was ready to go and complete a mission. Mother Mary opened her door "Now go and get these young recruits ready for the mission ahead. We will speak soon."

"Yes we will, I'll see you soon and thank you for taking the time to speak with me."

"Bye Merlin." Merlin turned and hurried towards the Great Halls of Knowledge.

Meanwhile Archangel Michael was making his way out into the Universe, he didn't really didn't like being out here all by himself, he felt vulnerable, he knew he had the power of the sword, but he still felt vulnerable, he had to keep his wits about him. The Universe is so vast, beyond any comprehension and the different astral levels all connected, but different.

"I'm feeling totally disconnected out here!" Archangel Michael said to himself. He could see Zeus and Thor in deep discussion now, they were not fighting any more. Odin approached them and sat himself beside them. Archangel Michael looked over to the left of them and there was Apollo talking with Artemis. Archangel Michael couldn't make out what any of them were talking about, no matter how hard he strained his ears to hear. "Well at least, there is a truce for now" Michael said to himself. Crouching down beneath a bit of debris that was just floating by, he managed to get a look from a different view and that's when he saw it, the blackness, it was indeed closer than he thought.

"Oh my goodness, there are thousands of them." Then as he was staring closer at this mass of blackness, there in the centre he could start to feel the power coming out of it and the sound of a low buzzing vibration.

"Hey you!" Archangel Michael turned around and saw Pan, God of wild nature.

"Pan! Ssshh!" Archangel Michael whispered.

"Why, what are you doing here?" Pan said climbing off of more debris and crouching down beside him.

"Can you hear that low buzzing vibration Pan?"

Pan turned his head to one side and listened, "Yep, that's been like that for a while, we have all heard it, but thought it was just the Universe echoing back at us". Archangel Michael rolled his eyes "Ok I'm going to show you something but I need you to be quiet and not tell anyone until I see you next time ok."

Pan nodded his head fast, he was eager and curious to see what Michael was going to show him. "Ok, just follow me, round the side of the debris."

Archangel Michael looked at Pan and nodded in the direction he wanted Pan to go. Pan did as he was told and followed Michael around the other side of the debris, the buzzing got louder as they crouched back down. "Now look, see that dark mass?" "Woah yes." Pan said his eyes had grown as big as saucers.

"Good, this is not the Universe's echo. This is the dark but you don't know they are right there, because they blend in, with the whole Universe. Only when you are looking from this perception can you see its form, look closely Pan and tell me what you see".

Pan held tightly onto the debris, whilst straining to see inside this huge mass of dark, and just for a second. "I see it, oh my thousands of people, oh no I've lost it!"

"Ssshh Pan, good I'm glad you saw them too, only for a second though, that happened to me too."

"Why could I only see them for a second?"

"That is because our vibration is too high, this is how they have managed to get so close, their vibration is low and slow."

"Why have they come Michael?"

"I'm not sure, which is why I have to report back to Merlin, and you Pan are not to mention any of this to anyone ok?"

"My lips are sealed, but when will you be back?"

"Soon Pan, very soon."

Suddenly Zeus stood up and shouted at Thor "Don't try and fool me, what do you take me for?" boomed Zeus, so much so the debris that Pan and Archangel Michael were holding onto shook.

"Time to leave before the fighting begins Michael or you may not make it back." Michael stood up and left as quickly and as quietly as he could.

When he got back he realized that Merlin was now having the meeting with the young recruits, so he decided to go find Mother Mary and let her know what he had found.

Chapter Nine
The Gifts

As Merlin got closer to the Great Halls of Knowledge, he could not only hear the rumble of excited voices, but he could feel the energy bouncing off the walls. Before he said anything he was going to have to calm this energy down a bit. If only he could find that wand of his. A quick twist of that wand and the energy would be neutralised, but now he was going to have to remember the magic spell to calm this energy down. "What was it, oh it's on the tip of my tongue, if only I could find that wand, how much easier it would be!"

Merlin slowed his walking pace down as he tried to recall the spell. Its no good, I'm just going to have to calm them down with my voice and my own energy. He was kicking himself for not remembering the spell and misplacing his wand!

Latecomers rushed past him as he entered the Halls, he noticed a few recruits that were preoccupied with some sweets, and they didn't even notice Merlin come in. Merlin smiled to himself, as he continued to walk towards a platform at the end of the Hall. He stepped up onto the platform and as he did, 'just like magic', it became quieter and the energy calmed, eventually it was so quiet you could hear a pin drop. Merlin was surprised, but that was the amount of respect everyone had for him, he was their elder, a wise, knowledgeable, kind, caring and compassionate man.

Merlin noticed Sophia sitting on the benches at the right side of him, and he noticed Zee directly at the front with some of his friends, Merlin was relieved that Sophia had showed up.

"Thank you all for your patience with me, I know you have been waiting over an hour for this meeting. Thank you also for your silence, I don't like to raise my voice if I don't have to."

Everyone laughed, there were a few voices and some coughs and then silence again.

"Thank you for coming, those of you who have decided to do this mission, thank you for stepping forward, without you we couldn't have moved forward at all. Those of you who have decided to stay behind, thank you, because without you here, keeping a watch on the young recruits and protecting our lovely home, we, as in the Senior Angels, Archangels and myself would not have been able to go and do our own mission on the Astral Planes. So, be proud of yourselves, whatever you have chosen to do."

"I'm not going to bore you all again with the reasons why this mission needs to take place, if any of you that want to hear it again, you can hear a recording of it, in the first Hall of Learning, it will be there, behind the lecturer's desk, and it will be there for 48 hours only. So, if you need to refresh your memory, before you step forward for this mission, I suggest you listen to my recording again. However, we should all by now know, that Planet Earth is in trouble and the dark forces are pushing their way forward to take over completely and this cannot happen, because the Earth will be out of balance and out of alignment with the Universe and will indeed implode. So we are sending you to bring Planet Earth back into balance and alignment. Your biggest, toughest job is to remain yourselves, keep shining your light and reignite the light in others and love unconditionally, all the while trying not to lose yourself in many illusions that others are living."

Another rumble of voices came from the recruits, and then once again quiet. Merlin couldn't help but be surprised that he didn't need his wand or a magic spell to calm such an excited crowd, he just needed to be himself.

"Thank you." he said quietly. "So this is the next step for you now to take, for those of you who have decided to go on this mission, you need to make your way to the Halls of Learning where you will be greeted by 7 Angels, each Angel will give you a colour on a card, the next Angel will give you a white feather, the third Angel will give you a number, the fourth Angel will give you a key, the fifth Angel will give you courage, the sixth Angel will give you unconditional love, the seventh Angel will give you hope. You will then find the table with the same colour as your card on it. There are 7 tables, one of the tables will have your colour, for you. When you match your colour to the table, look for your name, your name will be listed, and a Guide's name will be next to yours. This Guide will be with you throughout your human life. This Guide is there with you to help you, whenever you need it."

"Your Guide will then meet you at the table and you will spend time in the Hall getting to know your Guide, your Guide will tell you what to expect and how to connect to them, once you arrive on Earth. Once you have become acquainted with your Guide they will take you to the Departure Lounge where they will show you different dates and times and years, they will then ask you which date you would like to be 'born' on earth. They will then match you to Earth Parents and a country. You will get shown who your Earth Parents are and what you can do for them. How you can help them know unconditional love, compassion, patience and tolerance. However, be aware not all Earth Parents will be aware of your purpose and may reject your light and love. Remain yourself, remember they are living in illusion and have also had to protect themselves from hurt and pain. Once you agree, you will be connected to your birth name and date of birth. So we can then keep a record of each recruit and know where on Earth you are. Then your guide will take you to the waiting area, to be called. However, before any of this happens you are allowed to say your goodbyes to your elders and friends here, but you cannot stay for long, we need to activate this mission as soon as possible and our own barriers cannot be down for long. We cannot leave ourselves open for any kind of attack."

"Are there any questions so far?"

Zee put his hand up. "Yes Merlin I have a question."

"Go ahead Zee."

"What is the colour, white feather etc for?"

Sophia gently smiled, relieved she didn't have to ask that very question.

"Ah good question and thank you Zee for bringing it up". Merlin cleared his throat, "These are gifts, gifts given to you by us, and at some point you will need, use or have one of them. The colour is for two purposes, the first is for our benefit here, we need to know where each recruit is, all the time, so we can connect with you through colour. The second purpose is for you, a colour you feel you have a connection with, a favourite or lucky colour, this is your reminder, that you have a purpose where you are."

Merlin continued, "The feather will appear to you in times of sorrow, loss and struggle, when you are struggling in life, its our calling card, if you like, to let you know, you are not walking alone, we are here, walking with you. The feather will bring you comfort, in a time of despair. The number you are given, will show up in your life on a regular basis, some of you will call it your lucky number, some of you will put it down to coincidence, hopefully you will all be aware of your number at some point throughout this mission, this number is also a calling card, it's your Guide, trying to communicate with you, when you see your number come up, time and time again, become aware of the synchronicity and of giving you a sign when you don't know which way to turn or what to do for the best, your number will show up and your Guide will be trying to guide you at that very moment.

"Is everyone understanding so far?"

A resounding YES came from the recruits, but silence followed to allow Merlin to proceed.

"Ok, great. The fourth Angel will give you a key, it will be a key to knowledge and wisdom. Every single one of you have knowledge and wisdom within you, all that you have learned and experienced here so far, has given you the tools to use on this very mission. You will never forget this Knowledge or Wisdom, but you may not remember you have it, once you have incarnated into human form. The key will be incarnated with you and will stay within, until it is needed to open the door to knowledge and wisdom. In other words, once you begin to seek for knowledge and wisdom, the key will unlock the door within.

The fifth Angel will give you courage, there will be many times throughout your mission that you will need courage. Courage to be alone, courage to lose everything or someone, courage to love, courage to let go, courage to live, courage to die, courage to forgive, my, the list is endless, but with courage, anything is possible. You will have this courage living within you, you will feel it, when you have to use it.

The sixth Angel will give you unconditional love, here you have it and work with it all the time, but once incarnated you may lose it and use love as a bargaining tool. For example "I'll only love you if you do….. for me. If you don't … that means you don't love me. I did that for you, now give me what I want /need."

There was a murmur of quiet voices from the young recruits. A few looked at each other looking a bit puzzled. Merlin waited for the silence, and when it came he continued.

"I'm sensing a few of you, have never come across love like this before?"

Zee put his hand up, "Merlin can I ask another question?"

Merlin nodded. "Thank you Merlin, are you saying that this love you speak of is love? It certainly doesn't feel like love to me or to any of us for that matter, I mean we have never experienced this love, that you speak of and I don't think I will experience using this kind of love when I incarnate, I…"

"Oh my dear Zee, you most certainly will experience this kind of love, almost every human being on Earth is using this kind of love and it would be foolish of you to think you will escape it".

Zee feeling himself go slightly red, decided not to speak anymore. Sophia noticed Zee's flushed cheeks and quietly had a little giggle to herself, she had never seen Zee get flushed with embarrassment. As she looked over to him, the sun shone through the windows, and made the Halls look really bright, the sun picked out the blonde highlights in his hair. His embarrassment, made him look vulnerable, which made Sophia's tummy flip. There is definitely something about you Zee, I really like Sophia thought to herself.

Merlin carried on, "Ahem getting back to you question Zee. Is this love actually love? I would say to you it is a love that has been created on Earth, but it is not pure, it is not unconditional love, it is love with conditions. People of the Earth were born with unconditional love, but learnt, very quickly that they could bargain with it instead of the power of love, people began to love the power. So People of the Light and Dark have conditional love and a love of power which is another way of the People of the Dark taking over. However, you are all taking unconditional love with you and it will be within, just the same as courage, you will feel it, when you use it, the challenge is to recognise how it makes you feel when you use it and then step into it and use it always."

"Finally the Seventh Angel will give you the gift of hope, and again hope will live within you, it will always be there, because without hope, nothing is achievable, once you feel hope, within your soul, anything is possible. Hope will never abandon you. Hope is the one thing that can overcome your despair, if you let it. And you will need hope more than once in your incarnation on Earth. Hope can also activate your courage, it can activate all seven gifts as and when you are in need of them. Hope reminds you, that you are here on purpose."

There was a shuffling of feet and the young recruits started talking amongst themselves again. Zee started laughing and mucking about with his friends and Sophia tried not to keep looking over at him. He was such a jerk sometimes she thought to herself.

Merlin held his hands up and silence once again fell in the Halls. "I know I've just given you a lot of information so let's stop for a bit of lunch and lets meet back here at 2pm for the next instalment."

With that everyone got up, and started making their way out of the Halls their voices getting louder as they went. Sophia stayed sitting, watching everyone pour out of the Halls and thinking to herself that everyone seemed so eager and excited, even those that were staying, they felt ready to start doing something. Why can't I feel like that? Sophia held her cheeks with both hands, resting on her knees.

Zee was making his way out of the Halls now, still playing about with his friends. Sophia followed him with her eyes until he was out of sight. She was so focused on Zee, she hadn't noticed Merlin standing in front of her.

"This is getting a habit!" he said with a smile

"Eh?" Sophia replied.

"This, you sitting here, it's like deja vu, weren't you here on our very first meeting?"

"Oh yes I believe I was Merlin, and I have to add, I'm still no better off as back then, I still have no idea what I'm going to do". "Well sometimes Sophia it's better to choose to do nothing, and out of nothing, you would have made a choice, try that for a while, see what happens".

"Merlin, but I feel I need to do something! I'm so frustrated with myself right now". "Sophia frustration is not the word you need to use, you are having a battle with yourself and ego, you know there is a native American Indian proverb which goes something like this – there is a battle of two wolves inside us all, one is evil – it is anger, jealousy, greed, resentment, lies, inferiority and ego and the other is good – it is joy, peace, love, hope, humility, kindness, empathy and truth. What wolf wins? The one you feed. So my dear Sophia, which wolf of yours is going to win?" Merlin said as he stepped off the platform and walked out of the halls.

Sophia just stayed, cheeks of her face, in her hands, looking down at the floor. She was completely away in her thoughts, that she didn't notice Zee, who had come back into the Halls.

"Sophia," Zee screamed in a high pitched voice but smiling while he did it. Sophia looked up a little startled, but once she realised it was Zee, she looked back down at the floor. Zee plonked himself down beside her, gave her a little jab with his elbow and leant forward to get some sort of eye contact with her.

"Zee; what do you want?" Sophia sighed, sitting up.

"Well I wasn't earwigging or anything but I overheard you and Merlin talking and I was just curious to know the answer."

"The answer to what Zee?" Sophia said getting impatient and a little angry at him for overhearing their conversation.

---

* Two wolves, Native american proverb.

"Which wolf are you going to feed Sophia, I can't believe you haven't decided yet!" Sophia just looked straight ahead and she took a deep breath. "Can you just leave me to work it out by myself?"

"I can, but I don't want to, we all leave today, and I want to know if you are coming." Zee looked at her, you really do fascinate me, he thought to himself, still looking at her he asked her again more softly this time "Sophia, what are you scared of?"

"Nothing, absolutely nothing Zee, I just feel this is a pointless mission. My answer has not changed Zee, no matter how many times you ask." Sophia replied feeling quite agitated that she had to keep repeating herself.

Zee pursed his lips and said "Ok, I get that, I totally get that, but don't you think we should at least try to do something?"

Sophia ignoring the question, looked up at Zee, he was staring straight into her eyes. Sophia felt herself getting red, quickly she asked him "How comes you are so calm about it, does it not scare you, that you may get lost and become like those already there?"

Zee broke eye contact and looked at the floor. "Well I gathered that if you were there with me and I got lost, you would find me and steer me back to the purpose of us being there."

Sophia looked at him stunned, for a moment she thought that he was just messing with her, but as she looked at him, he remained serious, there not even a twinkle in his eye.

"You have got to be kidding me? I mean what makes you so sure I won't get lost too and what if our paths never cross, what if we all get lost? What happens then? Have you really seriously thought about this Zee?"

"You really have no trust in yourself do you? Or belief for that matter". Now it was Sophia's turn to look at the floor. "I totally believe in you Sophia, after all our classes, and how much you have achieved, the way you think, it makes so much sense and it's simple. I don't know anyone else like you, everyone comes to you for your knowledge and advice. You have helped me loads, in some of our tasks." Sophia raised an eyebrow, "I have?"

"Yes for sure, I just watched what you did and I did the same." Smiling Zee stood up. "We leave today and I want you to come with me, I've got to go and catch up with Abe, he is staying behind, but I want to see him before I go, so I'll meet you back at the Halls of Knowledge, you know it makes sense". He bent down and put his hands on Sophia's knees. "Trust yourself Sophia, you were made for this mission!" and with a squeeze of her knees, he made his way back out of the Halls.

I need a drink, Sophia thought to herself, and with that she walked out the Halls too.

Zee was out looking for Abe in the cherub gardens, when he saw Jazz sitting by a tree with her friend Sara. He walked over to them. "Hey, have you girls seen Abe, while you've been here?"

"No can't say we have, although I did see him earlier in the halls."

"Yeah, he was there, but then he disappeared." Zee said looking around the garden. "Have you seen Sophia, Zee?" Jazz asked.

"Yep, just now, I tried to talk to her about coming on this mission, but she is being stubborn".

Squinting looking up at Zee, Jazz replied "I was going to ask you if you managed to talk her into coming, I've tried too. I really don't think she is going to come".

Zee looked at Jazz "Oh I think she will come, she just needs a bit more persuasion, but I've got to find Abe, before I go back and talk to Sophia, so if you see Abe can you let him know I'm looking for him and that I'm making my way back to the Halls." "Yeah sure, good luck with Sophia, I will also talk to her again."

"Cheers, see you back at the Halls." Zee said as he turned and made his way back inside.

Abe was walking through the corridors towards the Sanctuary Room, when Zee called out to him. "Hey Abe, wait up". Abe turned round, and Zee jogged up to his side. "Hey!"

"Hey!" Abe replied with a small smile.

"Abe, I just wanted to let you know before I go, that I admire you for not going on this mission, that takes guts to not just follow your friends, and I wanted you to know that".

Abe turned to look at Zee. "Thanks Zee, that really means such a lot to hear you say that, I know a lot of my other friends are disappointed and I do feel like I've let them down, but I just couldn't go against my gut feeling."

"No need to feel bad mate, like I said I admire you."

"Are you scared Zee?"

"A little, maybe, I just feel as if we have to do something. We can't let the Earth implode, we have to try and stop the dark forces from taking over. I suppose I'm focusing on the job we have to do, once we arrive on Earth and I'm trying to not think about the what ifs."

"I have no idea, what to expect Abe, I've never been on Earth or had any experience with Earth people and their illusions, so I really have no idea, what we are letting ourselves in for. I just hope to Heaven, whatever it is, we succeed in our mission and get back home quickly!"

"Well I admire your courage Zee, I really do, and I hope for all your sakes, it is a success, and you all come home safe and well."

"Ah thank you mate!" Zee hugged Abe.

"See you back in the halls Zee, I'm just going to grab a drink."

"Well I'm going to try and find Sophia and have another chat, we need her to come on this mission."

"Has she still not made her mind up? Well good luck Zee, hope you can change her mind."

"Cheers mate, see you later."

"Yeah see you soon." Abe shouted out as Zee had already started to run back down towards the Halls.

With all the thinking that Sophia had been doing she was getting the start of a big headache coming on. I need a drink and I just need to switch off for a bit, I can't be doing with Zee trying to get me to come either she thought to herself. She found herself walking past The Sanctuary Room,

"Oh, peace and tranquillity, just what I need." She went in, poured herself a glass of water, and drank it down in one, she suddenly realised she was so thirsty. She walked around the room, checking to see if anyone else was with her, she looked in the pods and they were all empty. Good, she thought, even better if I'm on my own. She got inside one of the pods and started to relax and switch off. In no time at all, Sophia had fallen into a deep sleep.

Chapter Ten
The Journey begins

Everyone had started to make their way to the Great Halls of Knowledge. It was 2 pm and Merlin was already there waiting. As the Halls started to fill up with the young recruits, so the noise of excited chatter got louder. Merlin waited once again, until the last recruit had sat down, before he spoke.

"Welcome back," he said with that lovely smile, "I hope you have eaten and had something to drink."

"Yes!" came the different voices.

As Merlin scanned everyone with his eyes, he became aware that Sophia was missing, but he had to carry on, so he put Sophia to the back of his mind and continued.

"Ok, part 2. We need to send you on your way, so those of you who have chosen to do this mission, I suggest you go and say your goodbyes and just know this goodbye is not forever. You have an hour exactly to do this. The ones that have chosen to stay, please remain seated, I will take you through your mission process." There was excited chatter once more and the sound of benches and chairs being scraped along the floor as the recruits made their way out of the Halls to say their goodbyes.

Merlin waited for the Halls to settle once again and as he had thought, there were quite a few young recruits that were staying behind. They all sat looking at him, waiting for their next phase.

"My, quite a few of you here, I'm pleased you have decided to stay, you will be needed here, more than ever before." Merlin told them. A few shuffles in seats and a few coughs, and Merlin continued. "Your job will be to maintain contact with the young recruits Guides. Contact with the Guides is essential as we will need information from them to see how the young Angels are coping with life on Earth. Your job will also involve helping the Guides assist their recruits on to the right path, in case the recruit slips into the people's illusion. You will need to use your intuition more than you have ever done and follow with trust, the feeling it gives you. We will also need some of you to work alongside us, when we go and start our mission in the Universe. This will be explained to you nearer the time. We will also choose some of you to protect our walls and alert us of any incoming attack. It's going to be quite deserted here, while we are all doing our missions, and that leaves our home quite vulnerable. So as you can probably tell by now, by choosing to stay, you have a job just as big as the missions itself. Any questions so far?"

Merlin looked around the Halls, to see if anyone had their hand up. "No, good, I take it from the silence, that so far you all understand?" A few nods and mumbles from the recruits. "Excellent, let's move on, now what you all need to do is go to the Halls of Past, where you will be greeted by Archangel Gabriel".

"Archangel Gabriel works very closely with Mother Mary. She is concerned about the children's welfare and is often called upon to help the children of earth. However, she is also called to help the Earth Lightworkers and brings courage, confidence and communication. Archangel Gabriel will show you your jobs to do and refer back to her always with any concerns or new information, she will then inform Mother Mary."

The young recruits started to talk with excitement. "Ok…" Merlin said trying to get their attention. Silence fell onto the Hall. "So if you would like to make your way to the Halls of Past, you have time to stop to say your goodbyes to your friends, but don't be too long, Archangel Gabriel will be waiting."

Merlin stepped down from the platform, thinking to himself, where could Sophia be. It was so unusual for her not to be here. Merlin allowed the young recruits to leave the Halls and took a rest on one of the benches. Abe walked over to where Merlin was sitting.

"Ahem, Merlin?"

"Yes Abe, haven't changed your mind have you?" Merlin replied hoping that he hadn't changed his mind.

"No Merlin, not at all, but I was going to ask if we could stay with our friends until they go to the Departure Lounge?"

"Yes, yes of course you can Abe, no problem at all."

Abe smiled, "Thanks Merlin!" and he hurried and walked out of the Halls. Jazz was on a mission already to find Sophia, she couldn't see her anywhere in the Halls and wanted to know why she wasn't there. She was making her way outside to the cherub garden, when she spotted Zee coming in from the Cherub Garden.

"Zee, have you seen Sophia?"

"No I was going to ask you the same thing."

"Where would she be? Do you think she could be in the gardens?"

"Nope I've just looked all over the gardens, no one there, not even the usual crowd that sit under the cherry blossom tree, but I suppose everyone is saying their goodbyes and getting ready." Zee said a little despairingly, time was running out and he really wanted Sophia to go with him.

"Hey Abe," Jazz shouted seeing Abe, at the very last minute walking into the dining hall. Abe walked a few steps backwards to see who it was calling his name.

"Ah Jazz, what's up? Oh hey Zee".

Zee walked towards Abe "Have you seen Sophia Abe"?

"Nope can't say I have," he replied scratching his head.

"Where can she be?" Jazz said sounding very frustrated.

"She wasn't even at the second half of the meeting either, mmm do you think she is choosing to stay?" Abe said.

"No she can't choose to stay, she has to come with us so we need to find her, let's split up and see if we can ask others to look out for her too. She can't have disappeared." Zee said.

"I'll have a look in the Halls of Past, as that is where the ones staying have to go to meet Archangel Gabriel, she maybe there talking with Gabriel." Abe replied.

"Ok well I'm going to her room, to see if she is there and you Zee, go to her favourite window seat in the Halls, she may be there."

"Right and then meet back in the Halls of Knowledge, yes?"

"Yes Zee!" came two replies.

They all scattered in different directions. Abe made his way to the Halls of Past. He wasn't too keen on the Halls of Past, it was a reminder of his own past. The Halls of Past are full of every person's past, everything a person has done has been recorded and stored here, until the next incarnation, when they get moved to the Akashic records. The Halls of Past just keep a recording of one incarnation at a time, unlike the Akashic records, that has the actual blueprint of your soul and has records of each lifetime and incarnation. His last past life was not all that clever and Abe didn't feel it was his best incarnation. Maybe that's why he had chosen to stay behind. As Abe entered the Halls of Past, Archangel Gabriel was smiling at him.

"Hi Abe, are you ok?"

"Hi, well we are trying to find our friend Sophia, I don't suppose you have seen her?"

"No, sorry Abe, I can't help you."

"That's ok, I just need to go and tell my friends, she is not here, but I will be back." Archangel Gabriel chuckled, "That's fine Abe, go do what you've got to do, I'll still be here." "Thanks!" Abe was glad to be out of there to be honest, he didn't like the thought of his past showing up!

Chapter Eleven
Missing

Abe made his way back towards the Halls of Knowledge checking the Gardens one last time just in case she was there.

Jazz had searched everywhere and was getting quite concerned for Sophia. She decided to make her way to see Mother Mary, maybe she would be able to help.

Zee was back in the Halls of Knowledge and Abe called out to him.

"Any luck?!"

Zee turned to see Abe walking towards him.

"No, no sign of her anywhere, and time is running out, we have to leave soon."

"Shall we search her room and see if we can find Jazz too as we haven't seen her in a while either?" Abe suggested.

"Well that's all we can do Abe, I'll go to Sophia's room, you go to Jazz's room and hopefully between us we can find the pair of them. I'll check the Gardens one more time too."

"Ok Zee, we will meet back here then, yes?"

"Yes in half an hour because that's when we all need to be back here anyway."

Zee turned to leave the Halls and Abe followed. No more was said, but once outside the Halls Abe said, "Good luck!" as they went in different directions.

Mother Mary had been busy talking with Archangel Michael when Jazz knocked on her door. Mother Mary got up and answered.

"Jazz, what can I do for you?"

Jazz noticed that Archangel Michael was inside too and said, "Oh, I'm so sorry to disturb you Mother Mary, but we have lost Sophia, we can't find her anywhere and we wanted to know if she was coming with us or if she was staying and ...." Jazz stopped to take a breath.

Mother Mary said, "Oh my dear Jazz, no you haven't disturbed us and I haven't seen Sophia for a while either. I will go back and have a look for her as I need to find Merlin as we are getting close to your departure."

"Shall I come with you Mother Mary?" Archangel Michael asked as he stood up.

Jazz had forgotten how tall he was and his wings were just as big as he was.

"Jazz, close your mouth dear, you'll catch flies! Michael, stay here will you, just in case Merlin comes by or Sophia."

"Yes, of course," said Michael sitting down again.

"Right, where have you looked?" said Mother Mary closing her door behind her.

"EVERYWHERE!" Jazz replied despairingly.

"Have you checked the Sanctuary Room?"

"No, but I thought that would be locked up because we are all leaving?"

"No my dear, the Sanctuary Room remains open at all times because no one knows when one may need a little sanctuary," Mother Mary smiled. "Let's try there first."

Meanwhile, Zee and Abe found themselves back at the Halls.

"Well, anything?" Zee said looking at Abe with a bit of hope on his face.

"Nothing, and by that question I take it you didn't find them either?"

"Nope."

They both sat down on the wooden bench.

"Where can she be?" Zee said out loud.

"Mmm," replied Abe.

Mother Mary and Jazz arrived at the Sanctuary Room and opened the door.

"Anybody here?" Mother Mary said as she walked in, silence came the reply.

"Sophia!" Jazz shouted as she stared to walk around the room, she too was met with silence. Jazz looked over to Mother Mary and shrugged her shoulders. Mother Mary called out one last time, "Sophia, are you here?"

There was nothing, not even a murmur.

"Let's go to her room, she's not here, she would have heard us."

"Ok Mother Mary, but I have already been to her room," Jazz said, feeling disappointed. They closed the door, not realising that Sophia was fast asleep in a pod.

All the young recruits had started to make their way back to the Halls where Merlin was now waiting to take them down to the Halls of Learning.

Abe and Zee were talking to Merlin when Mother Mary and Jazz walked in. Merlin looked up as Mother Mary got closer.

Merlin said, "Sophia is nowhere to be found, Zee and Abe have looked everywhere!"

"Yes, so have Jazz and I and I really don't know where she can be. It's not like her to just go off like this."

"Well, there isn't much we can do now, I've got to activate this mission. We need to get the recruits into the Hall of Learning to meet the Angels at least," said Merlin. There was a little disappointment in his voice, he was inwardly hoping she would go on this mission.

"I agree Merlin. After speaking with Archangel Michael a while ago, we need to activate this mission as soon as possible."

"Ah, he came back with information for us, how bad is it?"

"I'd rather not discuss it here, let's get our young recruits off and we can talk about it once this mission is under way," replied Mother Mary as she looked straight into Merlin's eyes. That look was all that Merlin needed to know that it was not good out there.

Zee jumped up, "Does that mean we are not going to take Sophia with us?"

"Well not if she doesn't turn up in time Zee, no, we can only leave our shield down for a limited time. She will have a job to do here if she doesn't come in time though so don't worry," replied Merlin.

Zee realised that going on this mission without Sophia was not what he was expecting. Abe put his hand on Zee's shoulder, "It's ok Zee, I will look after her."

Zee suddenly realised his facial expression was giving away his own disappointment.

Turning to face Abe he shrugged his arm away from his shoulder and he said, "Yeah, I know you will!" He gave a laugh and went back to his cheeky chappie bravado. He sat back down and said, "Well, I'm ready, bring the mission on!"

"Yay!" Jazz said jumping up and down clapping her hands. "I'm ready too, let's do this!"

"Yes," Merlin replied, "I think everyone is here, so excuse me while I get some order." He then stepped up on to the platform.

Silence came like a Mexican wave, it started at the front near Merlin and descended all the way to the very entrance of the Halls. This still surprised Merlin that all he needed to do was to stand on the platform and without saying a word, silence would fall across the Halls.

"Thank you all for your silence, I take it that you are all here to take up the mission and become the Light Workers on Earth?"

"YES!" came from the recruits with excited energy rising.

"Ok then, can you all follow me to the Halls of Learning to meet your Angels." Merlin stepped down from the platform.

Mother Mary said, "Merlin, I'm going back to my room, I've left Archangel Michael there waiting for me. If you need me, send Abe to come and get me."

"Yes Mother Mary, of course, I understand once it is all done here, I will come to you."

"Thank you Merlin and good luck!" said Mother Mary as she left the Halls.

Merlin looked at Zee and Jazz and smiled, "Ready?"

'"Ready," Zee and Jazz replied.

"Follow me to the Halls of Learning please." Merlin lead the way out of the Great Halls of Knowledge.

The Halls of Learning were not as big as the Great Halls of Knowledge, but they were still a fair size. Instead of wall to wall, floor to ceiling shelves of books there was a wall full of shelves filled with files and files of tasks. The Halls of Learning were also set out like lecture rooms, with tables and chairs and a board for the Lecturer to write on. When the recruits were learning how to be compassionate, unconditional and empathic, life skills they needed for their mission, they also had tasks to fulfil. Sometimes they had several tasks to complete in a short space of time. The Halls of Learning challenged them mentally, emotionally and physically.

Merlin opened the big double doors and let the young recruits walk in. As Zee and Jazz walked in they were surprised by how many of them were actually going on this mission.

Jazz looked at Zee, "Zee, I can see my friends, Sara and Amelia, I'm going to go and see them while we wait for our Gifts."

"Yes, no problem Jazz, I can see my lot over there too," said Zee looking in the direction of the huge doors. "They are still laughing and joking about by the looks of it, but still keep your eyes peeled for Sophia, she may still turn up." He looked back at Jazz and said, "Well fingers crossed she does anyway."

Jazz raised her eyebrows, "Never lose hope Zee!" She turned and walked towards her friends, Nathalie had joined them too.

Zee stood alone for a while before joining the others.

Once everyone was inside the Hall of Learning Merlin closed the doors and walked towards the front of the room. Out of the crowds of recruits walked the seven Archangels.

The Archangels followed Merlin to the front of the Hall and once again, silence fell over the recruits who were now facing Merlin as he stood behind the Lecturer's desk. Merlin spoke.

"Well thank you again for being quiet. I really appreciate it." Merlin paused before he spoke again.

"We are nearly there, this is phase 2, you are all here to collect your gifts, meet your Guides and pick your 'ENTRY' date, in other words the date you choose to be incarnated on Earth."

You could hear a pin drop in the Hall, it was so still and silent. It was like everyone held their breath while listening to Merlin speak.

"'To my left are my amazing friends, the Archangels who will be giving you your Gifts. You have seen them before, but now I'm just going to introduce you."

"The first you see is Archangel Sandalphon. He is known by everyone as the TALL ANGEL." Everyone laughed as he was indeed extremely tall!

Merlin carried on, "His role is to listen and carry the prayers of humans to the heavens. He will be giving the Gift of the white feather to remind you that your prayers have been heard and you are never alone when you seem to be struggling with life."

"Next is Archangel Metatron. He is the keeper of the Akashic Records, he will present you with the key to all knowledge and wisdom within."

"Archangel Raziel is the Angel of Mysteries, the meaning of life, psychic studies etc. He is here to give you the Gift of Colour."

"Archangel Jeremial is the overseer of souls. He looks after souls that are waiting to reincarnate. He will be with you in the Departure Lounge, but he will also give you the Gift of Numbers."

"Archangel Chamuel is the Gatekeeper to the world and is in charge of world peace and a protector. He is here to give you the Gift of Courage."

"Archangel Gabriel is the Communicator and he will bring messages to you through thought and the spoken word. He is here to give you the Gift of Unconditional Love."

"And finally we have Archangel Raphael, the Guardian of the Tree of Life and the Divine Healer. He is here to give you the Gift of Hope."

"Now I will leave you all in my friends capable hands, if we could just ask you to create a line in front of each Archangel and collect your Gifts and don't forget your Guides will be waiting to greet you once you have your Gifts."

The recruits started to move into lines in front of the 7 Archangels and Merlin left as quietly as he could. The Hall started to slowly fill with excited chatter from the young recruits and the Hall echoed the excited chatter out into the corridors.

Zee and his group of friends stood in the line behind Jazz and her friends. There were so many recruits in front of them they couldn't see which Archangel they were seeing first, although they knew it wasn't Archangel Sandalphon as he was towering over everyone's heads and he was the third one down the line.

Zee kept turning around and looking towards the door in the hope that Sophia would walk in. Jazz was having an in depth conversation with her friend Nathalie and Zee's friends tried to get involved with playing pranks on each other.

Zee tried to calm his friends down, "Hey guys, come on, we are not here to play around we will be seeing the Angel soon. Come on, cut it out!"

"How come you are so serious all of a sudden, you were happy joining in earlier," questioned Pete.

"Yes I was Pete, but now we have got a mission and I'm feeling that we have to to be a bit more sensible."

"Fair enough, we were just trying to amuse ourselves while we wait, but I get what you are saying," replied Pete turning back to his friends.

Zee looked around the Hall to see if he could see any sign of Sophia. As he looked back at the queue he was standing in his eyes met Jazz. She was doing the same, scanning the Hall looking to see if Sophia had walked in. They both looked at each other and Jazz shrugged her shoulders and Zee pulled his mouth down into a sad face.

"Come on Jazz," said Nathalie, "we are moving!"

Slowly the queue got shorter and soon they were near the Angel. They could see who the Angel was now and it was Archangel Metatron. Jazz turned round to tell Zee, "It's Archangel Metatron Zee, we will get a key from him."

Zee just put his thumb up to say ok. He was having an inner battle with himself, half of him wanted to run out of the Halls and wait for Sophia to appear, but the other half was telling him he must leave today. It was making him feel a bit twitchy, he didn't know what to do for the best.

Now it was Nathalie's turn to receive the key. Archangel Metatron said something to her, but he couldn't hear what it was.

Jazz was next, she took one last look back at Zee and then smiled as she stepped forward. Archangel Metatron smiled at Jazz, he had a gentle energy about him, but there was also an undercurrent of strength.

"Ah Jazz, I'm glad you chose to join in on this mission. This key has everything you will seek, just remember it's there and you can use it as much as you want." He handed her a tiny key that was so small you could probably lose it is you weren't careful. Jazz decided that as it was so small and quite light she would put it in the top pocket of her coat. That way it would, hopefully, have no chance of falling out.

"Thank you Metatron, I will treasure it always."

"Good luck Jazz and we will be with you."

Jazz smiled and went to join the rest of her friends who were now queuing in the second line.

Pete pushed Zee to the front, Zee had been deep in thought and didn't realise they were next.

Metatron held Zee's shoulders, "Easy fella, there is no rush," Metatron said as he released his grip from Zee's shoulders.

"Sorry, I didn't realise I was so close!" Zee said, a little startled by Pete pushing him forward like that.

"Zee, you seem a little tense, are you sure you are ready to go on this mission?"

Zee looked up at Metatron. "Yes, I am ready, I just didn't think it would be without Sophia, I thought she would come."

"I'm starting to think you have got a thing for Sophia, don't you lads?" Pete said looking around at his friends. They all laughed in agreement.

Zee turned around and said, "It's not that Pete, I just thought that with her there it would be better for all of us, she is so switched on and she would know if we got lost or if the Dark Forces were trying to take us."

"But who is to say she will be with us, we could all end up in different places?"

"Pete, you would know when Sophia was around, you would just know it would be her, you would know her energy and she would draw you in. You would always want to be around her, she would make you feel safe and you would just know."

"Yeah well, where is she? She isn't even here, so we don't even have her coming with us so stop stalling Zee, get the key and move on, you're holding everyone up."

Zee looked back at Metatron, "Well you heard him, I guess I need the key."

Metatron took Zee's hand and placed a key into his hand and held his hand over it. Zee was surprised how heavy this key felt and it was ice cold.

Metatron spoke to him, "This key holds all you will need to know throughout your incarnation, the answers to your questions will always be within yourself. Your gut instinct will never fail you, just trust in it. Good luck on your journey."

Metatron let go of Zee's hand and Zee looked down at the key, it was an old iron key, nothing like Jazz's. He opened his jacket and put it in his inside pocket. He turned and looked at Pete. "Your turn," he said with a wry smile. He then looked up at Metatron and said, "Thank you, thank you very much."

"My pleasure."

Zee turned and joined Jazz and her friends in the next queue.

"This is the one who gives us our own colour on a card, he is called Archangel Raziel, he is the Angel of all Mysteries and psychic study and magical abilities etc," Jazz informed Zee.

"Oh, ok," Zee replied.

"What's your key like Zee? Mine is tiny, shiny and so light, I can't even feel it's there!" said Jazz, quite happy with her key.

"Well mine's the opposite, it's heavy, ice cold and is an old iron key, like the one we use to open the heavy gates to the Universe's space."

"Oh really? How strange!"

"Mmm, indeed," Zee replied, once again scanning the Hall looking to see if Sophia had come after all.

Jazz leant into him and whispered, "I don't think she is coming Zee."

Zee turned to look at Jazz and just smiled.

"Ooh, I'm next," said Nathalie to Jazz with excitement.

Jazz laughed, "Yes Nathalie, I know."

Nathalie stepped forward and Archangel Raziel gave her her colour which was red. Nathalie was quite disappointed as red was not her best colour, but Raziel explained she would need red in the life that she had chosen because red is the colour of strength and action. Nathalie felt a bit better, but still wished for a better colour. She walked away to the next line as Jazz stepped up to get her colour.

Raziel smiled at Jazz as he put the colour into her palms of her hand. It was the beautiful colour of turquoise. Raziel explained that this colour would help her in this life time to have courage, to be brave, to take chances, to never give up and to be dynamic. Jazz thanked Archangel Raziel, not quite understanding why she would need those things, but it didn't really matter because she loved that colour. She walked away looking at her colour not noticing that she was walking the wrong way.

"Er, I think you are meant to be going that way, you have been here," said another recruit who was queuing for his key.

"Oh," said Jazz and laughed. "Sorry, I was totally absorbed by my colour, ha ha!"

"No problem!"

Jazz walked towards Nathalie who was staring wide eyed at her.

"What," said Jazz.

"You," said Nathalie, "I'm trying to get your attention and you walk away from me."

"Sorry Nat, what colour did you get?"

"I got red," Nathalie replied, turning her nose up and opening her hand to show the colour on the palm of her hand.

"Oh Nat, it's a beautiful red though."

"Mmm, what colour did you get?"

"I got my beautiful turquoise." Jazz opened her hands to show her colour on the palm of her hand.

"Ugh, and I got red!" Nathalie said, slapping her hands against her sides.

Jazz giggled, "It's just a colour!"

"Yeah, right!"

It was Zee's turn to get his colour and he stepped forward to meet Archangel Raziel.

"Hello Zee, I'm pleased you came."

"Thanks Raziel, I'm glad I'm here," Zee replied with a smile.

Raziel opened Zee's hands and placed the colour blue, a sky blue, into the palms of his hands.

"This colour blue will help you in this life time to speak up for yourself, it will bring you peace whenever you look at it and will come with belief in yourself."

Zee gulped, he was very good at speaking up for others, but speaking up for himself was a different matter.

"I accept your gift Raziel, thank you."

Raziel cupped Zee's hands and said, "You are welcome." Zee turned and looked for Jazz in the next line.

It was now Pete's turn to step up for his colour.

"This is where we receive our white feather Zee, LOOK AT HOW TALL HE IS!!!"

Zee chuckled, "He sure is Jazz."

They stood patiently discussing their colours as they waited in line.

Merlin meanwhile, had been searching for Sophia to no avail. He decided to go and see Mother Mary and Archangel Michael to find out what they had decided and what the next plan of action was.

Soon it was Jazz's turn to collect her white feather. Archangel Sandalphon bent down and opened up her hands, palms facing upwards, her hands looked tiny against his.

Archangel Sandalphon placed a beautiful white feather in the palm of her hands and gently cupped them closed. He then spoke in a gentle soft voice.

"This white feather will appear many times in your incarnation and sometimes it will not be white, sometimes it will be a different colour. This is our calling card letting you know that your loved ones in heaven are close by. This feather is also a sign to let you know that in your times of struggle or despair we are with you, we never left."

Jazz looked down at her hands and then looked up at Archangel Sandalphon.

"Thank you Sir."

Archangel Sandalphon smiled and started to stand up. Jazz had forgotten how tall he was while he was bent forward talking to her and as he stood up she felt tiny once more.

She turned and looked at Zee and just whispered, "Wow!"

She then walked over to where Nathalie was standing. Nathalie was still feeling disappointed with her colour. She looked at Jazz and said, "Do you think I can ask for a different colour, I mean, I'm not ungrateful or anything, but I'm not connecting with this colour."

Jazz giggled, "Oh Nat, you are still not happy? I don't think we can change our colours, they have been given to us for a reason, we just don't know what that reason is yet and you may incarnate and fall in love with that colour. If I was you, I would just accept it, it will all become clear once you incarnate I'm sure."

"Huh, in what way do you think it will become clear Jazz?"

"Oh, I don't know Nat, may be that colour will be a trademark where all the other Light workers on their mission will recognise it or something like that. To be honest I have no idea, but you haven't been given that colour for no good reason, that I know for sure."

"Mmm, I suppose," said Nathalie now looking at her feather.

Zee was next to meet with Archangel Sandalphon and wow was he huge. Zee felt suddenly intimidated by his size and looked down at the floor. Archangel Sandalphon bent forward and lifted his chin up until their eyes made contact.

"Hey fella, don't stand in my shadow, stand tall and shine, don't be fooled by my size I'm as soft as marshmallow really!" Archangel Sandalphon gave Zee a wink and Zee smiled.

"That's better fella, now here open your hands and take this feather."

Archangel Sandalphon repeated the exact same words as he had done to all the other recruits who had gone before him. "This is a sign to remind you that you are not alone, this feather will appear when you are seen to be struggling or in despair."

Zee closed his hands gently around the feather and looked up at Archangel Sandalphon who was now standing up again. He thanked him and walked to the next line.

Nathalie turned round to him and smiled, "That was an experience wasn't it? I've never seen anyone that tall before."

"Yes it was Nat," Zee replied.

Jazz then turned to Zee, "And this one is Archangel Chamuel, he….."

"I know Jazz, he will give us courage."

"Oh, I didn't think you could see," said Jazz giggling. "Can't you tell I'm a little excited!"

Zee smiled, "Oh, indeed!"

Zee felt quite flat, there was still no sign of Sophia. He had been discreetly looking round for her while they had been going round the Halls.

"We are next!" Nathalie squealed.

"Oh my days, I can't wait!" Jazz squealed back.

Zee rolled his eyes, he couldn't understand their excitement. It wasn't a usual task, this was a mission.

Nathalie stepped forward to be greeted by Chamuel. Pete walked over to join Zee with his other friend Shane.

"Which Angel have we got now Zee?" Pete asked.

"Archangel Chamuel, he is going to give us courage."

"Oh yeah, that's right."

"You alright Zee, you look a bit down."

"Yes Pete, I'm fine, I just think I'm getting a bit tired."

"I know mate, it is taking ages."

It was Jazz's turn to step forward, Archangel Chamuel took her hand and spoke in a kind and gentle, but strong voice.

"I'm going to give you the Gift of Courage. You will use it many times during this incarnation. I want you to never forget you have it, it will be with you always. Archangel Chamuel then lifted Jazz's hand and placed it on his stomach and then moved her hand on to her own stomach.

"Courage lies within, you will feel it when you need it."

Jazz felt a rush of energy that made her stomach have a butterfly feeling. She also became a little light headed. Archangel Chamuel let go of her hands and smiled, "Good luck on your mission."

"Thank you," Jazz replied and looked round for Nathalie. She was standing in the next line looking a little dazed by what had just happened and didn't even notice that Jazz had joined her. Neither of them spoke.

It was Zee's turn to step forward. Looking up at Archangel Chamuel he opened his hands up to receive his Gift of Courage.

"Ah," said Chamuel, "I don't need your hands for me to place your Gift. I don't need you to touch Courage, I need you to FEEL it."

Zee looked at Chamuel wide eyed as he took his hands and placed them on his stomach. Zee felt a tingling sensation through his hands and then Chamuel moved Zee's hands to place them on his own stomach. Zee once again felt a strange tingling sensation go from his hands into his stomach.

"Courage lies within you, you will feel it when you need it, you will feel it within your stomach area." Chamuel gently let go of Zee's hands and stepped back. 'Good luck on your mission Zee, and don't forget Courage comes from within."

"Thank you Archangel Chamuel."

Zee turned and walked towards Nathalie and Jazz who were still stood in silence. They all acknowledged each other, but no words were spoken. They were all absorbing the Gift of Courage.

Soon it was Nathalie's turn to step forward to meet with Archangel Gabriel, still no one spoke. Nathalie stepped forward. Zee was surprised to see Pete and Shane standing behind them, but they too were very quiet, not talking. That was a powerful Gift, Zee thought to himself.

Nathalie stepped away from Archangel Gabriel and nearly tripped over Jazz.

"Sorry," Nathalie said.

"No problem Nat, I'm not concentrating myself."

"Jazz," Archangel Gabriel called in a soft gentle voice, holding out her hand.

Jazz stepped forward and took her hand. Archangel Gabriel looked deep in Jazz's eyes and placed her hand over Jazz's heard.

"Oh Jazz, don't let life make you hard, always keep your heart open and let the love flow out. This is the Gift of Unconditional Love, feel it always, use it always and give it away as much as you can."

Jazz's eyes stung with tears as she became overwhelmed with this beautiful Gift. It felt so pure and powerful.

"This Gift is not just for others, it is for you also, love yourself always, no matter what."

Tears fell on to Jazz's cheeks and she closed her eyes as the feeling of Unconditional Love poured into her heart.

"Unconditional Love lies within, you will feel it when you need it." Archangel Gabriel took her hand away and Jazz opened her eyes.

"Thank you Archangel Gabriel."

"You are welcome Jazz, good luck on your mission."

Jazz stepped away, wiping her tears. She had a brief glance to see Zee as she went to find Nathalie in the next line.

Zee followed Jazz with his eyes just to make sure she was ok, she looked really upset. A little apprehensively he took a step forward and placed his hand into Archangel Gabriel's.

"Hello Zee, how are you feeling so far?" "Yeah, I'm ok thank you," Zee replied.

"Mmm, you words do not match our heart's energy Zee, are you denying yourself or someone else you love? No need to answer the question to me, but don't kid yourself Zee, honour your feelings. You already know the answer to the question."

Zee looked at Archangel Gabriel stunned, he wasn't sure how he felt in that moment and then it hit him like a train. I'm in love with Sophia! Realising his face was telling Archangel Gabriel all she needed to know, he pulled his hand away and shuffled his feet.

Archangel Gabriel smiled and whispered to him, "It's ok, it can be our secret, as long as you honour your feeling yourself, no one else needs to know."

Zee looked up at Archangel Gabriel and once again took her hand. Clearing his throat he said, "I'm ready."

Archangel Gabriel placed her hand on to his heart, "This is the Gift of Unconditional Love, feel it always, use it always and give it away as much as you can. This Gift is not just for others, it is also for you. Love yourself, no matter what. Unconditional Love lies within, you will feel it when you need it."

Zee took a deep breath in and felt as light as a feather, he was completely absorbed by the power of Unconditional Love, he could feel its vibration in his own heartbeat. He breathed out slowly still looking at Archangel Gabriel and said, "Wow!"

"Good luck on your mission Zee and remember, stay true to yourself."

Zee smiled and replied, "Thank you Archangel Gabriel."

Zee stepped away from Archangel Gabriel and turned to Pete, "Your turn, brace yourself!"

Pete looked at Zee to see if he was joking, Zee kept a straight face and walked away. Pete stepped forward and took Archangel Gabriel's hand.

Zee joined Jazz at the next queue. It was Zee's turn to tell Jazz who the next Angel was.

"This is Archangel Raphael, he will give us the Gift of Hope."

"How do you know that already?"

Zee laughed, "Because I saw him as I was walking towards you and I thought I would tell you first for a change."

"Oh, ok!" Jazz replied.

"Ha ha ha, Jazz I'm playing with you, don't take it personally! I'm just having a laugh with you, I don't mind that you tell me who we have next."

"Sometimes Zee I just don't know how to take you!"

"What? I'm just joking" Zee chuckled.

"Yeah, well sometimes it's the way you say it!"

Nathalie interrupted their conversation, "Man, I'm thirsty, are we going to have to wait too much longer, I could really do with a drink!"

"It looks like you will have time to go grab a drink from the water fountain that's just outside in the corridor, but if you want a tea or juice you may have to wait," Jazz said.

"Nat, go now, we will keep your space," Zee said.

"Really, ok great, I won't be long."

"It's ok, go!"

"I'm sorry Jazz, I didn't mean to tease you," Zee said looking at Jazz and pulling a sad face. "Friends?"

"Of course, how could I not be friends with you?" Jazz said smiling at him, she gave him a nudge with her elbow.

"Give us a hug," Zee replied with his arms open.

Jazz hugged him tight. She silently hoped he would be near her on this mission, she could do with a friend near to help her and support her.

Nathalie came back a little out of breath. "Hey did I miss anything?"

"Only a hug, but if you want one…" Zee opened his arms.

"No it's ok, I'm too hot for a hug, but thanks for the offer."

"Here we go, we are next," said Jazz stepping forward.

"Not long now!" Nathalie replied.

Archangel Raphael stepped forward and took Nathalie by the hand. Nathalie turned to look at her friends who were standing behind her. Zee put his thumbs up as if to say it was ok.

Nathalie turned and looked at Archangel Raphael.

Zee and Jazz stood together in silence for a while and then Zee stared to once again look around the Hall with his eyes. His eyes fell back to Jazz. She looked at him, shrugged her shoulders and said, "She's not coming."

Zee just nodded, he knew, but he still had hope.

Nathalie stepped back and looked at Jazz wide eyed, "That was amazing, you will love him!"

Jazz giggled, "Ok Nat, meet you in the next line."

Archangel Raphael took Jazz's hand and she stepped forward.

"Jazz, my Gift to you is the Gift of Hope, you will always have Hope in this mission, there will be times where you will feel hopeless, you will feel less Hope, but when you feel this I want you to remember the Gift of Hope I gave you and it will be with you always. Use it, keep hold of it and never let it go. The Gift of Hope means the absence of despair. Hope is the consciousness of strength and encouragement."

Archangel Raphael then placed his hand on Jazz's heart and Jazz felt a warm, comforting energy. She felt a little dizzy and her heart had a few palpitations. Archangel Raphael took his hand away and smiled, "You will be just fine Jazz, you are strong."

"Thank you Archangel Raphael." Jazz turned and walked away.

"Ah Zee, are you ready to step forward?"

Zee stepped forward, "Yes, I'm ready."

Archangel Raphael took his hand, "This is the Gift of Hope and I can feel you already have this in your heart, you are indeed hoping for something at this very moment."

"Er, yes, yes I am!" Zee said surprised that Archangel Raphael could actually feel it.

"Never give up on hope Zee, without it nothing is possible. Hope will carry you through this mission, you will use Hope more than most, but it will never let you down."

Archangel Raphael took his hand and placed it on his heart, Zee closed his eyes, and he could feel the energy of Hope absorb into his body. He took a deep breath in and as he slowly breathed out he opened his eyes.

Archangel Raphael took his hand away and said softly, "You will be ok Zee, trust your instincts always and never lose Hope."

"Thanks Archangel Raphael."

"You are welcome Zee and good luck."

Zee stepped back and turned to walk towards Jazz. When he got to Jazz he realised he was thirsty and he needed a drink.

"I'm going for a quick drink, I'll be back in a min, save my place!"

"Hurry Zee, this line is moving fast!"

Zee didn't hear, he had already made his way out of the Hall. There was a long queue for the water fountain so Zee decided to go to the one just inside the main entrance. Just as he got there he saw Merlin walking in. The huge doors and tall ceilings made Merlin look quite small in comparison and it wasn't until Merlin was almost next to him that he realised that Merlin was quite tall really.

"Ah Zee, have you finished receiving your Gifts?"

"Er, not quite, I'm on the last one, which is the Gift of Numbers, but I'm a bit confused as to what to do next as I thought you said when we get to our Colour our Guide will be there to choose our Date of Entry to Earth."

"Well that's right, did that not happen then?" asked Merlin, slightly confused himself now.

"No, we got our Colour, but then went to the next line?"

"Ok, I'm going to need to come and find out how they are doing this. Carry on, have your drink, I'm going to the Hall to find out what's happening."

"Ok Merlin, I'll be quick."

"Take your time Zee, no rush honestly, we have to get this right!" Merlin said as he walked hurriedly away.

Jazz and Nathalie were busy talking to Pete and Shane about what numbers they would get and what was so magical about a number when Merlin burst into the Halls and told everyone to please stop whatever they were doing for a second.

"I just need a quick word with Archangel Raziel as we have young recruits who are a little confused and to be honest, I am a bit confused too, so allow me to find out what's next and I will enlighten you all. Please Archangel Raziel can I have 5 minutes of your time?"

"Of course," Archangel Raziel said stepping down from his platform, "What is it?"

Merlin pulled him to one side and then spoke, "I'm a little confused and also concerned that I have told the recruits the wrong thing. I thought that when they came to you they received a Colour, their Guide and then they chose their Date of Entry and parents etc before heading to the Departure Lounge."

"No, no, this is true, but only after they receive all their Gifts, once they have all their Gifts they come back to this table. We thought this would be the best way as….."

Archangel Raziel looked around and used his arms to express himself, "As you can see, there are a lot of recruits here and to get all their Guides in here too would make it a little cramped so we thought we would do it at the end and go by Colour so, in other words, everyone with the Colour red can stay and meet their Guide while everyone else can take a break. Then we will call them in Colour by Colour."

Merlin took a deep breath and said, "Oh yes brilliant, ok well I need to explain this to the recruits so they know what to do. Ok, Raziel, go back to your place and continue, I will just make this clear to the recruits and we can carry on."

Archangel Raziel walked back towards his table and Merlin walked towards the centre of the Hall. In a loud voice he just asked for a bit of silence which he received almost immediately.

The Wake Up Call

He smiled as he noticed Zee just walking in through the doors, "Just in time Zee."

Zee made his way back to the line where Jazz and Pete were waiting. Merlin continued to tell everyone that once they had received all their Gifts they would get called back to table 2 Colour by Colour. They would then meet their Guides and pick their Date of Entry, their Earth parents and siblings.

"And now please continue. If you have any questions please ask your Archangels or me."

Everyone started to talk amongst themselves again and Merlin left the Hall. He was still hoping to bump into Sophia to find out what she was going to do.

Jazz and Zee were now back in line waiting to be give the Gift of a Number.

"Eek, it's all getting a bit real now," Nathalie said squeezing Jazz's arm.

"I know!" Jazz said. "It really is!"

Zee just remained silent, deep in thought.

It wasn't long before Nathalie was called up to see Archangel Jeremiel.

"Last, but not least," Nathalie said as she stepped forward to greet Archangel Jeremial.

"Welcome," Archangel Jeremial smiled.

Nathalie felt at ease straight away.

Jazz was looking at Zee who seemed to be far away somewhere in his mind.

"Hey," Jazz said softly. Zee jumped a little.

"Sorry didn't mean to disturb you out there, are you ok?"

"Yeah, I'm fine Jazz, just thinking."

"Hope not many what ifs are in your thinking?"

"Eh?"

"What ifs? You know, what if this happens, what if I can't make it, what if I lose myself? You know, what ifs!" Jazz replied.

Zee chuckled, "Oh those what ifs, yeah well I've had plenty of those today!"

"Haven't we all!"

"Yep, but clearly we are not paying attention to those what ifs because we are still waiting for our Gifts!" Zee said with a little humour in his voice.

"Clearly," said Jazz and as if on que Nathalie stepped down from Archangel Jeremial's platform.

"Well, that's it for me, I suppose I'll meet you all again in the Departure Lounge because you all have different Colours to me."

Jazz gave Nathalie a hug.

"Ok Nat, take care, see you soon!" Jazz replied feeling a little tearful.

Zee stood with his arms open and Nathalie hugged him.

"You will be just fine Nat, go smash this mission!"

Now it was Nathalie's turn to get tearful as she stepped away from Zee, she looked up at him and said, "See you around Zee."

"See you around Nat!" Zee put his thumbs up and Nathalie walked away.

Archangel Jeremial was standing patiently waiting for Jazz to step forward, but Jazz was still watching Nathalie walk away. Zee nudged Jazz in the back, "It's your turn, go!"

Jazz jumped forward, "Oh ouch, that hurt a bit, sorry Archangel Jeremial, she is my friend and I just wanted to say goodbye."

Zee chuckled, "Sorry Jazz I was just trying to make you aware that Archangel Jeremial was waiting for you!"

Archangel Jeremial took Jazz's hand, "It's completely fine, now let's get on with it shall we?"

"Of course, I'm ready."

"The number I'm going to give you is the number 11, this is going to be a special number for you in your mission on Earth. It will be a way for us Angels who are trying to comfort you to remind you that we are forever present. Whenever you see the number 11, remember we are present and your prayers are being answered."

"Wow, thank you Archangel Jeremial, I hope I remember once I incarnate."

"You will know something when you see the number 11 appear all the time, you will search for a meaning and you will find it. Now go and good luck on your journey."

"Thank you Archangel Jeremial," said Jazz as she turned to Zee, "This is really it!" Her eyes filled with tears and she gave Zee a tight hug. She whispered to him, "This is harder than I thought and Sophia is not here."

Zee gulped hard, "Hey we are going to be ok! This is not goodbye, it's a see you later, ok, just remember this!" He continued to stay in her arms until he felt his own tears fade. As they both released the hug they looked at each other and smiled.

"Go get 'em Jazz, shine your light!"

Jazz still felt too emotional and just nodded as she let go of Zee's hands and walked away.

Zee gave a deep sigh and walked towards Archangel Jeremial.

"Are you ok Zee?" Archangel Jeremial looked concerned.

"Yeah, I'm cool, that was not easy though."

"I'm sure it wasn't," Archangel Jeremial replied. "Shall we get on with it?"

Zee looked up at Archangel Jeremial, he had a kind face with really kind eyes.

"Yes, let's do this!"

"Good, ok, the Gift I'm giving to you is the number that will show up a lot during your mission. This number is just to remind you that you are on a mission and you are not alone, we are with you. The number I'm going to give you is the number 7. It's not something I can physically give you, but it is already imprinted in your mind and once you see a 7 regularly it will trigger a feeling. Hopefully, you will make a connection with it in one way or another."

"Thank you Archangel Jeremial, I do feel very blessed to have all these Gifts and to have all of you walking with us."

"Never doubt it for a second Zee, we never left you and we will never leave you, just you remember not to walk away from us, stay true to you."

Zee flung his arms around Archangel Jeremial and hugged him really tightly. Archangel Jeremial stroked the top of his head and whispered, "You rock my friend, you will be just fine."

Zee stood back and quietly said, "Thank you."

Zee walked away, leaving Pete a little apprehensive about Archangel Jeremial and the whole mission.

"Pete?" Archangel Jeremial put out his hand towards him. Pete took it. "I'm ready!" he said.

Once all the recruits had their Gifts, Archangel Raziel summoned everyone who was given the colour red to the table to meet their Guides and for the next phase.

Nathalie had stayed in the Hall as her colour was red, she was joined by her other friends. Nathalie met her Guide and he was a Native American Indian Chief and his name was Running Water. He would be with her throughout her mission. She liked him and he made her feel safe and protected. She chose to enter Earth on the 13th November 1963 to parents in England. Her Dad was a hard worker, but a bit of a wheeler dealer type of man and her Mum was good and solid, but strict. She had no siblings.

She chose these parents as they would teach her strength, courage and independence. Nathalie felt this would help her on her mission to help others. Her independence would make her a great leader of Light and Love.

Her friend Celine chose to enter Earth on the 9th April 1961 to parents in Ireland. She would have siblings, a brother and 2 sisters. Her Guide was to be a fairy called Radella who was from the faery realm and would always protect her and listen to her inner thoughts.

Zee's other 2 friends also had the colour red given to them. Shane and Jake were at the table waiting for their Guide and to choose their Date of Entry before entering the Departure Lounge.

Meanwhile Jazz had gone back to Mother Mary's room to see if she had had any luck in finding Sophia.

Zee walked back to his room, he needed some time alone and to have a little peace and quiet for a while.

They never saw each other again, not even in the Departure Lounge, but they both hoped they would find each other once on the Earth for all their sakes.

Chapter Twelve
The Departure

Soon it was time for those with the colour turquoise to come to the Hall. Sara and Amelia went to find Jazz, who had just left Mother Mary's room. No one had seen Sophia. Jazz met Sara and Amelia in one of the corridors.

"Hey Jazz, come on it's our turn, we've got to go!" shouted Sara with a little nervous excitement in her voice.

"Really?" Jazz said, "Wow that was quicker than I thought." The three of them started running towards the Hall of Tasks.

Once inside they joined the queue to meet their guide. Sara and Amelia went first, while Jazz just waited for her turn quietly. Glancing around every now and then to see if Zee was hanging around or if Sophia was in the Hall, Jazz was beginning to feel a little anxious about the mission now and now her own "What if's" were going on in her mind. Thinking to herself, she tried to gain a bit more positivity. All of a sudden her name was called "Jazz". Jazz looked up and Archangel Raziel was beckoning her over to the table. She saw her name, next to her colour. She saw her Earth name and then her Guide's name Aris, and as she looked up, there she was a beautiful Egyptian woman.

"We finally meet," she said.

"Yes," was all that Jazz could say.

Aris smiled, "Shall we choose your date of entry and parents before going to spend some time together?"

"Yes," Jazz replied.

Aris laughed, "Ok then, you need to stop looking at me and focus on these dates, which ones are you drawn to?"

"Oh," Jazz laughed nervously and could feel herself going red. "I'm star struck, I'm sorry, you are so beautiful."

"Well thank you very much Jazz, however, there is more to me than my beauty." "Yes I'm sure, anyway dates, let's focus on some dates" Jazz replied trying to get back on track. Jazz started to scroll through the dates.

"Oh my there are so many! I mean how do I choose?"

"Well what era do you want to help? What you need to think about is this mission is happening now and it's getting worse on Earth not better. So I would probably choose anywhere from 1945 onwards."

"That helps a little, ok this date keeps coming to me, 24th November 1969 so that can be my date of entry."

"Ok brilliant, you were quicker than I thought you would be." Aris smiled "Now let's have a look at your possible parents."

There were quite a few to choose from, but Jazz had decided on a couple that were creative, strong and gifted musically. She was to have two siblings come after her, a sister and a brother. Straight away Jazz wondered if that would be Nathalie and Zee, she hoped it would.

"Let's go take a walk, I have much to talk to you about and you need to ask me lots of questions, and we don't have much time!" Jazz agreed and walked with Aris out of the Hall.

Soon enough all the Turquoise group had been seen and were getting to know their Guides. Now it was time for the colour Blue to make their way back to the Hall of Learning. Pete knocked loudly on Zee's door, "Come on mate, they are ready for us!" Zee jumped up from his bed and opened the door, "Already?" he said a bit dazed as the knock on the door had actually woken him up from a deep sleep.

"Yes, it has been two hours Zee, where have you been?"

"Two hours! I must have fallen asleep straight away, ok hang on I got to grab my jacket, it's got the gifts in it!" Zee picked his jacket up and flung it over his shoulder and shut his door. "Why are you looking at me like that?"

"Like what?"

"You still look half asleep Zee, are you sure you are with me?"

"Yeah, I'll be alright in a minute, just a bit fuzzy headed that's all." The two of them walked towards the Hall of Tasks, in silence. As they got closer they could hear the buzz of excited voices, who were already there waiting.

"Wow I didn't realise there would be so many of us with the same colour!" Pete said as they entered the Hall of Tasks. "Neither did I Pete" Zee replied scratching his head.

They both walked towards Archangel Raziel, "Hey fellas, are you ready to meet your guide?"

"Is there no queue then Archangel Raziel?"

"No, not at the moment, I think everyone is just saying goodbye to each other first, because you go off to the Departure Lounge with your Guide after here and you will be at different departure gates, unless of course you pick the same entry date as someone else, but usually this is the last chance you get to say goodbye to your friends."

Zee and Pete looked at one another and then gave each other a hug.

"I'm gonna miss you Zee, try and find me yeah?"

"I'm gonna miss you too Pete, and if I don't find you, you will have to find me."

"I hope we do meet and become friends on Earth, it will be good to have someone with me."

"Yeah mate I feel the same." The pair of them just stood in silence for a bit, hugged again and then Zee said, "Well let's not put it off any longer, let's do it."

"Wait, let me go first, at least I won't have to watch you go, let me go first."

"Fair enough, Pete it's all yours mate."

Zee stepped to one side and bowed to Pete, as he stepped forward, Pete paused, turned to Zee, "See you later Zee!"

"See you later Pete!" Zee replied with a wink.

Pete stepped up to find his colour, and next to it his name. He then saw his Earth name and then his Guides name. His Guide was a warrior, a protector, and he would look after him in this lifetime. His name was Arrow.

Pete liked Arrow from the start, he had the same sense of humour and liked joking around.

"Ok Pete, let's find out what date of entry you are going to choose." Pete looked at the different years, 1947, 1952, 1959, 1965, 1968.

"1968, I think." Pete said.

"Ok now a date", Arrow replied.

"Erm, let me look, let me look, erm….ah 5th August."

"5th August 1968, you sure?"

"Yep, I'm sure, why? Is that not a good date?" Pete asked Arrow, now doubting himself.

"No, I just want to make sure you are happy with the date Pete, it's so difficult for your Earth Mother to adjust, if you decide on a different date once you have connected to her, and it can be dangerous for you both."

"What do you mean?"

"Well just say you choose the 5th August as your date of entry, but once you have connected to her soul, with your soul in her womb, you decide you actually want to enter Earth on the 20th August instead, or even worse the 1st July, it becomes quite a shock for the Mother's body to adjust, and it could be dangerous to your life and your Earth Mother's life. So I'm just being thorough, and I'm making sure you are sure, of your choice."

"Oh wow, it's more complicated than I thought! Well, I'm certain I won't change my mind, 5th August 1968."

"Great let's have a look at parents and sibling." Arrow said showing Pete film images of different potential parents and siblings, if any at all.

Zee had just been standing quietly watching everyone, with their Guides and every now and then he would look at Pete and smile. Thinking to himself that he really hopes to meet with Pete in this lifetime, he will miss him a lot.

"Zee!" Archangel Raziel quietly called.

Zee looked over at Archangel Raziel and pointed in at himself and mouthed, "Me?"

"Yes, you!" Archangel Raziel smiled.

Zee walked over to him. "Is it time already?"

"Yes Zee, it's your time, go find your name with your colour, your Guide will be there to meet you."

"Okay," Zee replied as he walked towards the table. As Zee started to look for his name, he was surprised at how many names were on the list boy, this is going to be one hell of a mission he thought to himself. "Found me!" Zee exclaimed a little surprised to see his name on the list, he was half expecting it not to be there, because of his indecisiveness earlier that day. He looked across and discovered his Earth name and as he moved across he found his Guide was called Sewang he was a Tibetan Monk and he was to empower Zee's life on Earth.

Zee looked up from reading and there in front of him was Sewang. He was a lot smaller than Zee but he had the kindest face, and huge hands. "Wow!" Zee said. Sewang bowed and replied, "It is a pleasure to be here, working with you."

"I hope it will always be a pleasure Sewang, and that we become good friends."

"We already are!" Sewang replied with a wink. "Now let's have a look at which parents you would like to have in this incarnation." Sewang scrolled through many images.

"Now let's have a look at what date of entry you would like to enter Earth on."

"Ok," said Zee feeling butterflies in his stomach.

"Let's start with the year, which year would you like, bearing in mind, it will take you at least 20 years of your Earth life, before you realise you have a mission to complete."

"Oh really? Why so long Sewang?"

"Well you have to enter Earth as a baby, although there are other ways, but they are for the more evolved, and I don't want to get into that now, we haven't got the time. So for you and others on this mission you have to enter Earth as a baby, this will leave you with no memory whatsoever about here, but as you start to grow and experience your life, as you 'grow' through 'years', eventually you will start to question why am I here, this will be the start of your wake up call. The trouble with this, is that many of you, won't know how to pursue the question. You will need courage and hope to find the answer, which will be within and you have the 'key' to the answer, then once you find the answer, you then have the courage to act on it.

In other words answer the call." Saweng looked at Zee, "I've gone a bit deep haven't I? Did you understand any of that?"

Zee chuckled, "Oh yeah I did, don't worry about how I look Saweng, I always look confused when I'm concentrating." Saweng started laughing and he had quite a contagious laugh and Zee couldn't help but to start laughing too.

"Very good Zee, very good," Saweng said still chuckling and shaking his finger at Zee. "I'm going to like working with you, now where were we?"

"Well you were explaining we enter Earth as a baby and we don't remember why we have come to Earth, but after some years, we start to question 'why we are here' and this is our wake up call, but some of us won't recognise that we are indeed here on purpose, but all we have to do is remember that the answer is already within us, and remember that we are actually holding the 'key' and also remember that we have courage within us to act on the answer, which is to be the Lightworker and spread love into the Earth so the Earth becomes in balance with its own natural state of being."

"How did I do?"

"Zee you probably said it better than I did that is exactly what I meant."

Zee chuckled, "Told you I was concentrating."

"Ok, so let's get on with it, choose your date."

"Well if I want to be on Earth at the same time as my friends, what year will be best for me?"

"Mmm, some may be older than you, some around the same age and some younger."

"Yes, but if I choose 1975 for instance and my friends have chosen 1948, what's the chances our paths will cross?"

"Ok I see that you mean, well if it helps most of your friends have chosen between 1954 and 1975 so maybe choose somewhere in the middle."

"Erm I'm going for 1966, no wait erm 1968, yes 1968."

"You sure Zee?"

"Yep 1968."

"Ok good, let's tap it in, ok now which day and month?"

"There are too many to choose from!" There was a long silence as Zee was scrolling through so many dates.

Eventually Saweng spoke, "I'm not usually allowed to influence you at all, but if you ask for my help I may be able to give you a clue."

Zee looked up to see Saweng smiling at him, "Saweng , why didn't you tell me that before! Can you help me please?"

Saweng chuckled, "Sure can, it may help you to know that your friend Pete has chosen the 5th August 1968."

Zee smiled broadly, "Really?"

"Really," Saweng replied.

"Okay let me look at August 1968."

Zee started to scroll through all the numbers in August, he landed on the 20th. "There it is my date of entry is 20th August 1968." Butterflies filled his stomach again. "Let's tap it in, now wait for your boarding pass, it will tell you what gate to go to for your departure."

Zee tapped in his date of entry and waited for his pass to come out. "Here it comes, ok, now it's official, the 20th August 1968, gate 7."

"Put it in your jacket Zee, we don't want to be losing it, now it's time to choose your parents, do you need another clue?" Saweng asked with a twinkle in his eye.

"Do I need a clue?" Zee said looking puzzled.

"Well you may, if you are thinking of your friend Pete?"

"Ok, I still don't understand, but please give me a clue?"

"So you want my help?"

"Yes, can you help me?" Zee said despairingly.

Saweng laughed, "Yes of course, now your friend chose parents who live in England."

"Oh! Now I get it, ok I need parents in England, hey but what if they move to another country after I'm born?"

"Well you will both have something in common when you cross paths."

"Ah ok awesome, this is quite complex, it's not straight forward is it?"

"No Zee, it is not but we are managing well enough."

"Ok parents in England, wow, my days, there are lots!"

"Indeed, keep scrolling."

Zee stopped at a young couple who had just got married, were very much in love and hardworking. "Mmm, how about these?"

"Well how do you feel, when you look at them, and what do you think you could give them, and what qualities could you take from them?"

"I feel like they are my friends, but I'm not sure I could give them anything and qualities? I think they are the same as mine anyway."

"Ok so move on Zee, these probably are more likely to be your friends, they need a new Angel to teach them, how to be good parents."

"Ok, let me look…." Zee landed on an older couple, they already had 3 children, a daughter and 2 sons. They seemed solid, committed, strong, wise and knowledgeable. Everything Zee needed to learn on Earth, and they loved their children very much. "These, I want these people to be my parents."

"Ah very good choice Zee, they are older and will guide you well, you have siblings too?"

"Yes maybe with them I won't feel so alone and maybe they too are there to help me."

"Maybe or maybe not Zee, don't expect it to be anything at all, some are just on their own journey, bear that in mind. So are you sure it's these people?"

"Yes positive, I get a good feeling from them."

"So it is then," Saweng replied tapping the couple into Zees boarding pass card. "Is that it then?"

"Yes that's it, let's take a walk, I have much to tell you before we get to the Departure Lounge."

"Ok Saweng, whatever you say."

They both walked out of the Halls of Learning and headed towards the Departure Lounge. Jazz and Aris were on their way to the departure lounge too. Jazz was holding her boarding pass tightly. 24th November 1969, Gate 6.

"Wow," said Jazz "I didn't realise we had to go underground."

Aris smiled, "Where did you think the Departure Lounge was?"

"Well I always thought it was the building in the far corner of the Cherub Gardens."

"Oh the Reunion Hall," Aris said.

"The Reunion Hall?" questioned Jazz

"Yes that's the Reunion Hall, wherever you reunite with friends and loved ones, once your job on Earth is done. There is a hospital there too, if you come home injured, ill, or suddenly your soul has to recover, so you stay in the hospital a while."

"Oh, how strange that I always thought it was where we depart from."

"Yes, it's actually an Arrival Lounge, there is also a Dream Room, and a Contact Room."

"What do they do Aris?"

"Well the Dream Room is where we can go and visit our friends and loved ones, while they are sleeping on Earth. We visit them in their dreams to let them know we are ok, and also to see them, we miss them not being here with us, so it gives us a chance to see them and be with them a while; and the Contact Room is where we can send them messages and little signs to bring them our love in their time of despair."

"How lovely," Jazz said imagining herself in the contact room, writing a message of comfort to a loved one.

"Well when this mission is over, you will be arriving in that Reunion Hall, but for now you are leaving and we need to go to the lower levels, underground."

"Why do we need to go underground though Aris, how come there isn't a Hall or place above ground for us to leave from?"

"That is because my dear Jazz, you are a Light Being and where you are going the energy is dense and much heavier, there is a gravity on Earth, which is really strong and heavy. As we go down these stairs you will start to feel the change, it's ok though, you are perfectly safe, there is nothing to be scared of."

As they reached the top of the stairs, Jazz noticed how wide they were and that there were ten steps at time, there were no windows and although well lit, it looked darker than outside. A draught came up the stairs and reached Jazz's ankles, she gave a little shiver.

Aris giggled, "Honestly, it is ok, we got to go down to the basement, before we can get to Earth. Once you get into the Departure Lounge you will be fine it's a lovely place, bright and warm, let's just get this bit over with shall we?"

"So will I start to feel heavy Aris?" said Jazz, hesitating before she took her first step down.

"Yes, yes you will, you cannot enter Earth at this level of vibration, it's too high, so by going down these stairs, you lower your vibration, to match Earth's vibration. However, once you arrive back home, your vibration will lift back to the vibration you have now, so try not to worry too much."

"Ok, let's just do it!" Jazz said finding the courage to take that first step. As they both took the first flight, in silence, Jazz could feel the heaviness in her feet. Aris asked her if she was feeling ok and Jazz just nodded. Soon they were one flight away from the bottom.

"Phew may I say, this is exhausting, I feel completely drained." Jazz said.

"I know and understand completely, but your body will adjust to its new vibration quickly, you won't feel like this forever." Aris replied taking Jazz's hand. "Come on one more flight and we are there!"

Just as they reached the double doors into the departure lounge, Zee and Saweng were at the top of the stairs, and Saweng was having the same conversation about the heaviness and lower vibration. Zee hesitated, "What's the matter Zee? It's just stairs, it's safe to go."

"I know that Saweng, it's just….I thought Sophia would have at least made the effort to come and say goodbye, even if she didn't want to, I'd have thought she would have, you know, wished us luck or something, I just don't understand, and now we are here, it's happening, we are going, it would have been nice to have had the chance to say goodbye to her, that's all."

"I understand your wanting her to come Zee, however, there has been no sign of her, for a while and we are running out of time, there is only so long we can be open for, time is of the essence."

"Yeah I know," Zee sighed.

"Shall we get on with this then?" Saweng asked.

"Yep, let's do it!" Zee replied as he took the first step down, he was shocked at how the energy changed even on the first step. They continued walking down the stairs in silence, although Zee's thoughts were loud enough, for Saweng to hear them, Saweng was not going to tell him, he would remain silent.

Zee's thoughts were all over the place and only thinking of one thing, Sophia, where was she and why hadn't she come to say goodbye? Zee was so focused on his thoughts, he wasn't aware of how heavy his body had become. They had reached the double doors.

"Ready?" Saweng asked Zee.

"Ready," Zee replied. Saweng opened the double doors and they both walked through.

"Oh my days," said Zee as he looked all around, walking backwards and turning around trying to take it all in. The Departure Lounge was huge, high ceilings, bright and airy, and loads of recruits, souls, people walking about, some were sitting chatting, some were just sitting in silence, some were on their own, while others were reading.

In front of Zee was a huge screen with dates of entry and gate numbers with information on different times of entry. The gates were all around the Departure Lounge 1 – 12 were all on the left and 13 – 33 were on the right. To the right in the distance, Zee could just about see Jazz chatting away to her Guide.

"I wonder where Pete is?" Zee said quietly to himself.

"So many people!"

"Yes Zee, not all are going on a mission some are here to experience their own journey, to evolve their soul further."

"Oh, so some here are not on the same mission as us?"

"Correct."

"How can I tell who is with me on this mission and who has another purpose?"

"You will know, something will connect with each of you, just trust it."

"Mmm ok, well if nothing else I hope Pete and Jazz find me."

"Well let's wait and see, you may not realise how far away, you can be from each other, so don't put too much expectation on an outcome."

"Ok," sighed Zee, starting to feel a little lonely.

"Hey, I'm with you and will be with you all the time, just don't forget that yes?"

"Yes, I know, there's lots to think about though, isn't there? I mean…."

"Watch out! Ooo nearly fell over her!" Saweng shouted.

"I didn't see her, she is fast asleep too!" Zee said looking down at a young lady asleep on the floor.

"She probably missed her date of entry, and now has to wait for her time to enter again."

"So she will choose a different date?"

"Yes she will have to choose a different date, same gate number though."

By now the two of them had reached gate 4 and there were lots of people standing, waiting to board. There were two Guides at the front, checking their boarding passes, and leading them through to the waiting room on the other side.

Zee looked down at his boarding pass ticket.

"I believe we started at the wrong end, my gate number is 7, which is on the right hand side of the entrance. We automatically turned left."

"Oh yes, we did, didn't we?" Saweng said. "Ok no problem, let's walk a bit faster, we will make it in time no problem."

Zee and Saweng started to walk a bit faster. Zee didn't know if it was his imagination or not, but it felt like the Departure Lounge had got busier, and noisier.

Meanwhile, Jazz and Aris had reached their gate number and Jazz recognised Sara and Amelia from the Hall of Learning. They were more Nathalie's friends, but she was happy they were at the same gate as her. Jazz needed to sit down for a while, the heaviness of the lower vibration was making her feel very tired. She found a seat and Aris sat next to her on the floor. Amelia and Sara carried on chatting to their Guides.

"Oh how come I feel like this, when everyone else is feeling ok Aris?"

"It's because you are more sensitive to the energy shift Jazz, this will serve you well on the Earth. They will be more sensitive to the heaviness, once they have entered Earth."

"Well I feel totally exhausted by it."

"Which is why you will sleep well, once you arrive, because you are adjusting now, the others will be more restless as they haven't adjusted to the heaviness, so they will take longer to settle."

"Thank goodness for that, I'm needing to sleep now!"

"Well you can't, because it's nearly time."

Jazz looked up, she was sure that she just saw Zee walking past quite fast, but he was gone, before she had a chance to shout out to him. Puffing out her cheeks, she breathed slowly out. Her thoughts wandered to Sophia, she wondered where she was and what on earth she was playing at, she was sure that Sophia would have come to say goodbye at the very least. Jazz stood up and started to look around, just in case Sophia had decided to come late!

"I don't think she is coming," Aris said gently.

"No, I know, but I can't help but hope that she may have changed her mind," sighed Jazz, sitting back down.

There was a sudden cheer from gate 5 as the gate had just opened and everyone started to go through the gate to the waiting room.

"We are next Jazz, we won't be long." Aris said.

"Yes, not long before I can have a sleep!" Jazz replied stretching her arms above her head. "Boy, I feel really heavy."

Zee and Saweng finally reached their gate 7.

"Great, look at the size of that queue!" Zee exclaimed.

Saweng laughed, "Well it gives us an opportunity to have a sit down, there's no rush, come let's sit on the floor over there." Saweng said pointing to a quiet corner.

Zee sat down and suddenly the heaviness came to him. "Oh my days, I feel so heavy, what is that all about Saweng? I don't think I can get back up!"

Saweng laughed, "Finally it hits you! I was wondering when it would get you!" he said still laughing at Zee.

"Well it's got me, that's for sure, I can hardly move, Saweng I'm in trouble mate, seriously!"

Saweng couldn't move for laughing "Stop Zee, you are too funny!" Saweng was holding his belly.

"Well I'm glad you are finding it funny, I feel totally steamrollered! Give us some help!" Saweng laughed even more.

"Zee just wait for a minute, I can't help you, just rest a while."

"Saweng, I'm asking for help, I'm not going to be able to get up, if I rest, I'm going to get stuck here."

By now Saweng had tears rolling down his face and his belly was aching from laughing so much. "Ok, ok, just wait I've got to compose myself Zee."

Zee just sighed, he was not finding this amusing whatsoever. Jazz stood up to stretch, if she sat there for much longer, she would fall asleep and she certainly didn't want that! Suddenly she thought she saw Abe, amongst the crown of people in gate 5, and then he appeared again, he was looking for someone by the looks of it.

"Abe! Abe!" Jazz started to walk over to gate 5, calling his name, only for a worried Aris to run after her.

"Jazz! Jazz come back, we might be called, Jazz!"

"Abe!" Jazz screamed.

Abe looked across and saw Jazz. "Jazz!" they both ran to each other and hugged.

"I've been looking for you everywhere and Zee, have you seen Zee? I can't believe I nearly missed you!" Abe said as he hugged Jazz again.

"Yes I'm sure I saw Zee go past my gate, so he must be further down, I'm so pleased, we have got to say goodbye, have you seen Sophia?"

"Ok I will go find Zee in a minute, Sophia, no, no sign of her, I'm a little worried as we have looked everywhere no sign at all!"

"Jazz!" Aris called beckoning her back to gate 6.

The Wake Up Call

"Oh Abe, I've got to get back to my gate, listen if you catch up with Zee, tell him I said good luck and if you do get to find Sophia, tell her from me that she needs to get her bum on Earth pretty sharpish, we need her!"

"I will Jazz," Abe said hugging her tightly, "take care of you, and I'll be watching over you always, never forget that."

Tears stung Jazz's eyes, "See you later Abe, love you."

Aris took Jazz's hand, "Come on we have to go."

Jazz stepped away from Abe and gave a wave, "Bye," she whispered and turned to walk towards gate 6 with Aris.

Abe walked past gate 6, scouring the lounge for Zee, hoping he gets the chance to say goodbye and relieved he found Jazz. Saweng held out his hand to Zee, "Come on, on 3, ready 1, 2, 3 goodness Zee, you are like a dead weight!" he exclaimed as he managed to pull Zee up into standing position.

"I feel like a dead weight Saweng, I've never felt like this in my life."

A cheer from gate 6, it was their turn to go through to the waiting room. Zee and Saweng looked at each other.

"Not long now for us," Zee said.

"No, not long at all," Saweng replied.

"Ah well I need to stretch my legs, let's walk to the back of the queue."

"Ok if you want to".

"I do, but oh my, it's an effort to walk!"

"Don't start me off again Zee, my belly still hasn't recovered."

"I don't even mean to be funny."

"Which makes it even more funny! Now don't start, let's just get to the end of the queue."

"Hey, I'm sure that's Abe, that just walked past. Hey! Abe! Abe!"

Abe carried on walking, he couldn't hear Zee calling, as gate 6 were really cheering and laughing.

"Ah never mind Zee, look out for him, he has to come back this way," Saweng reassured him.

Zee reluctantly joined the queue. Maybe Abe had come to tell him, he had found Sophia, or to say goodbye, he was definitely looking for someone he thought.

They stood in silence for a while until another cheer from gate 6 broke their silence. "Why do they keep cheering?" Zee asked.

"Oh it's because there are friends that have joined them. The waiting room is now open, see, there they all go."

"What happens, once we get into the waiting room?"

"Well, you wait until your parents are ready for you and then you get called, then you stand in a column of light and it takes you to your mother's womb and then on your date of entry, you enter Earth."

"How long am I in the womb?"

"Depending on how late you enter the womb, but usually no more than 7 days."

"Ok, yes I can do 7 days."

"Zee, knowing you it will be just 1 day!"

"Mmm you are probably right, I don't like this heavy feeling."

"You will be fine, I promise, hey isn't that your friend?" Saweng nodded in the direction of Abe just walking back past gate 8.

"Yes! Abe! Abe!" Zee ran over to him, they both hugged.

"I'm so pleased you came Abe!" Zee said smiling.

"Thank goodness I found you Zee, I was getting into a right state, thinking you would have gone and I never got the chance to say goodbye."

"Oh mate, it's been really busy here and so much information and stuff to learn and then bam, we are here."

"But you are a sight for sore eyes, have you seen Jazz? Or Sophia?"

"Yes I saw Jazz, she said to tell you good luck, but no sign of Sophia, Zee I'm sorry."

"Ah that's ok, not going to worry about it anymore Abe, I can't, I'm leaving in a minute, I've got to focus on my own journey now."

"True Zee and if I see her I will look after her, while you are gone, I promise."

"Thanks Abe, can't believe you made it to say goodbye." Zee hugged Abe again. Gate 6 closed with a bang and all was quiet from over there.

"Well I suppose that's Jazz gone, your turn next."

"Did Jazz have gate 6 then Abe?"

"Yeah, a bit of a rowdy bunch!" Abe chuckled. "But Jazz will be just fine."

"Yep, she will, she's strong, I hope I get to meet up with her." Zee said daydreaming. The sound of a cheer and gate 7 opening brought Zee back with a jump.

Saweng touched Zee's arm, "Here we go".

Zee looked at Abe "I'm going to miss you!"

"Me too, but it's not forever, and like I told Jazz, I will be watching you always."

"Group hug?" Saweng said.

"Group hug!" Abe and Zee said together.

"Ok well I've got to go, as I may be needed by Merlin and it doesn't look like you will be here for long, the way the queue is moving!"

"Yep, I don't think it will take long Abe."

"So, see you later?"

"Yes, for sure Abe, see you later."

"Take care of you and good luck Zee."

"Thanks mate." Abe turned and walked back towards the double doors. Zee followed him with his eyes until he was completely out of sight. Zee and Saweng remained silent again for the rest of the wait.

Jazz was now in the waiting room with Aris, and was getting a little restless.

"Calm down Jazz, you don't want to enter Earth early and you are starting to make your Earth mum a little anxious."

"How? How can she be anxious?"

"She can feel your energy Jazz and once you connect with her in her womb, she will feel you even more."

"Really, she can feel me already?"

"Yes of course, Jazz, she feels you as a baby kicking and moving about."

"Wow that's amazing!"

"So don't get restless, you don't want to enter Earth too early, as you will have a fight to stay, you have to adjust in that baby body first and get used to the heavy vibration. You choose your entry date, let's stick to it!"

"Ok Aris, I think I understand, I'll calm down."

"Good girl, just relax, we won't be here long."

"I'm a little scared Aris, which is why my energy is all over the place."

"Jazz, you are going to be scared, this is the unknown, and many like you are also scared, but I am with you always."

Jazz smiled and squeezed Aris' hand.

Zee and Saweng were nearly at the doors of the waiting room, when Zee's friend shouted out to him, "Zee, see you on the other side."

Zee turned round to see Jake and Luke walking past. "Alright lads, I thought you had gone already?"

"Bloody missed our date, didn't we?"

"Oh no, you've got to wait here then?"

"Yep, until another date comes up, I'm at gate 5 and Jake is 6."

"Ah Jazz was at gate 6, if you get to meet up with her, look after her!"

"No worries at all Zee, and good luck mate." Jake said, putting his thumb up.

"Same to you guys, see you later!" Zee replied and with a quick wave of his hand, Saweng and Zee stepped into the waiting room.

It was a short while later that Zee got called to stand in the column of light and get ready to enter Earth.

"Well Saweng, this is it, I'll hope to remember you are with me."

"I'll always be with you Zee."

Suddenly Zee felt immense pressure at the top of his head and it was pushing him upwards, the column of light seemed to be moving upwards really fast, making it quite noisy and the pressure became really intense, he started hearing voices, and the pressure eased and a different smell, and a gasp of air, he had entered Earth.

Some time later, it was Jazz's turn to enter Earth, it took all the strength she had to remain calm.

"I just want to get on with it now Aris, I'm bored of waiting, I just want to be there already."

"I know and it is nearly time Jazz, I promise."

A few hours later, Jazz was called to stand in the column of light, Aris gave her a reassuring smile, and her date of entry began.

Soon everyone had gone and apart from a few delayed entry dates, the Departure Lounge was empty.

Chapter Thirteen
Courage

"Where are they?" Sophia exclaimed, bursting through Merlin's door. Merlin turned around somewhat startled, "Where are who? And where have you been might I add?"

"The recruits, where are they? I can't find Jazz or Zee anywhere, or anyone, where are they?"

"Well where have you been Sophia, they have been looking for you!" Merlin replied while gathering himself back together again. No one had ever just burst into his room like that before, it unsettled him a bit.

"Ugh, I fell asleep in the pod, in the Sanctuary Room, I must have slept all day, I woke up about 20 minutes ago and everywhere is empty and so quiet. So are they in the Halls of Knowledge, I did look there briefly, didn't see anyone so…"

"They have gone Sophia," Merlin said looking over his glasses at her.

"Gone? What do you mean gone, gone where?"

"Gone on their mission Sophia, they had to go, we didn't have time to wait for you."

"No!" Sophia wailed now sitting herself in Merlin's big armchair, tears filling her eyes.

"I never said goodbye, I never.." Tears overwhelmed her and she started to cry.

Merlin knelt down beside her and stroked her head. "I'm sorry Sophia, they did try and find you, even Mother Mary and I looked for you, they were just as upset as you, they so wanted you to go with the or at least say goodbye."

"I was so tired, Merlin my head hurt, it was never my intention to sleep all day, I just needed space, oh Merlin, I've let them down!" Sophia started to cry again.

"Now, now, come and dry those tears Sophia, you haven't let anyone down my dear!" Merlin said passing Sophia some tissues.

Sophia took some, "Thank you," she said through her sobs. She blew her nose. "I didn't think it would be that quick, Merlin, I mean, I thought they would be leaving in a few days time, not actually leaving today."

"Sophia, they, you, had plenty of time to think about whether you wanted to do this mission and we had to act quicker than we originally planned, as the dark forces are coming closer, we couldn't postpone this mission once and for all."

Merlin passed Sophia a glass of water.

"Thank you Merlin," Sophia whispered softly, slightly more composed. "I feel bad Merlin, I spent too long not knowing what to do, and now my friends have gone, I feel like I've abandoned them, but also I still feel like they have gone on a mission that is pointless, these dark forces, are very manipulative, and they can take control of my friends."

Sophia gulped down more tears, "My friends will get lost, and then what Merlin?"

Merlin knelt down in front of her again and held her hand. "My dear Sophia, I explained all of this in the first meeting. This mission will not be an easy one, however, I also said that we will be watching over you all, all of the time, I also said if you can recall, that if you are seen to be struggling we will send you signs to let you know we are still with you, and if the mission gets too tough for you, we will call you home."

"Yes I remember all of that Merlin and I've taken it all in and I understand we are there to help the Lightworkers who are there already".

"Yes, you see the Lightworkers who are there already are now becoming tired, the dark forces are overwhelming which is why we are now needed to bring the Earth back into balance, we cannot destroy the dark, but we must not let them take over, because our whole Universe will be in grave danger and even the dark forces, don't understand that now, they are controlled by greed and power."

"And that is what scares me about doing this mission Merlin, what if the majority of people on Earth, are already taken by the dark forces and are living an illusion, we are going to have a hard job trying to make them see, they are there for a purpose, a reason, and on top of that, not get lost on our way. Oh Merlin, I just couldn't bear it, if I lost my friends." Sophia started to cry again.

"My dear Sophia, let me explain something that I didn't mention in the meeting. Earth is the centre of the universe, the people living on Earth as human beings have forgotten why they were originally there. You see, there has always been opposites, since time began, but the centre of the Universe has always existed.

When the Universe imploded in on itself, the Planet Earth was born, or created whatever word, you wish to choose, and it was created with only love on it, in its present form. Earth has everything it needs to live, air, water, earth, wind and fire, and something else that all humans have forgotten about."

"Which is?" Sophia asked curiously.

"Its heart," Merlin replied.

Merlin stood up, his knees cracking as he did. He poured himself a glass of water and sat down on a sofa that was opposite Sophia.

"Earth has a heart?" Sophia questioned Merlin. Merlin gave a little chuckle surprised that Sophia seemed surprised by this new information.

"Yes Earth the Planet has a heart." Merlin replied.

Sophia sat up a bit more, in her comfy armchair, "Where is the heart Merlin?" Sophia whispered as if no one should know about this.

"Well," Merlin said taking a sip of his water before sitting back in the sofa, "It's deep within the Earth's centre, so deep that it can never be destroyed. But it beats, every minute continuously and as it beats it sends out a vibration of pure unconditional love, all over itself."

"How very beautiful Merlin."

"Indeed, now what happened was that souls from all over the Universe came to Earth, to experience this pure unconditional love in human and animal form."

"They were living the Earth's heartbeat through their own heartbeat and would experience what this unconditional love felt like. Their own hearts connected to the vibration of the Earth's heart. As the vibration of love got higher and stronger, it started to attract darker forces from other parts of the Universe and they became curious. So they also came to Earth and what they witnessed was that love was a power that was so great with it anything was achievable and anything was possible."

"However, this love can never be bought. Soon the greed for the power of love was taken over by greed for control and power over the people. The Dark forces thought this love had control and power and they wanted it. This started to bring imbalance and fear. Human beings started to hide their power of love and started to love with conditions and attachment. Human beings soon forgot the power of love and began to love the power, and became attached to things outside of themselves and they became more attached to the lower vibration of superficial world of materialism."

"There are now very few human beings that show this unconditional love all the time, but every now and then human beings show humility and humanity by helping others as well as animals. Human beings believe their first basic instinct is survival, this is true, if it is you on your own, drowning in the sea, you fight to survive. However, the first basic instinct is not survival, the first basic natural instinct comes from love."

"How many human beings would jump into that sea to save the person drowning, without giving any thought to their own safety or life? How many human beings today have run into a building on fire to get others out?"

These people then get called heroes, and their response is 'I just did what anybody would do.' There is the power of love in action. Only when the brain kicks in and logic follows does it stop you from helping another person, and even then when we feel helpless and sad, we say a prayer, and hope they get out safely."

"If we had lost love as our natural instinct, we would not pull over our cars and run towards a car accident, these acts of random kindness are coming from the love vibration. Love is a powerful source and anything is possible with love as a foundation. With the negativity that has built up over the thousands of years, Earth's heart is still beating, however, its vibration is getting weaker. Which is why I have called you young recruits to this mission. Your mission to help wake these other Earth Angels up, to open their hearts once again and connect with each other and the Heart in Earth, and become strong with the love vibration."

"You know what the word love stands for don't you Sophia?"

"No Merlin, I'm not sure I do."

"Love means: Let Our Vibration Expand."

"Wow Merlin, do the others know this?"

"No I thought I would leave that for you to share, once you decide to do this mission, you let them know, Love is the only way and let them know they have to expand that love vibration and no longer fear it, step into it, embrace it, only then will the dark forces start to retreat."

"The vibration of love needs to be projected out far and wide. We need to bring back the balance of the Universe and not allow the Dark forces to take over. You all have a job to do and the message of love to give, every person on Earth has a purpose, they matter very much, they have greatness within them. Their light is dim, we need them to shine, they are good enough and they are loved and we here are so proud of each and every one."

"Oh Merlin do you really believe we could make a difference?"

"Sophia if you make a difference to one, it's one more than we have and remember, there are plenty of recruits that are now already on their way."

"But do you think or believe we can actually be successful in our mission?"

"Sophia, if I didn't believe it was possible, I would never have asked you, young recruits to do this mission, but I believe in you all, and I believe you all can achieve this mission as difficult as it maybe and as challenging as it can be, I truly have every faith that we can win!"

"Oh Merlin, my heart is saying to go, and my head is telling me all different things and I'm not going to lie Merlin, I am still really scared."

Merlin smiled, "It's ok to be scared Sophia, but don't allow that to stop you from being the greatest grandest version of yourself, don't allow it to sabotage who you could be, be scared, but work with that feeling."

"What if I fail Merlin?"

"Ah there's the ego again, failure is not bad, it just means there's another way, a better way, it doesn't mean you are useless, thick, stupid, not good enough, it just means there is a better way, don't allow the fear of failure stop you either."

Sophia let out a heavy sigh. "How long have I got? Before I make up my mind."

"Well we have a few recruits that missed their date of entry and a few late arrivals, they will be going in 2 days, we can only leave our barriers down for a few hours for our own safety. So if you do decide to go, you will need to let me know by morning, so I can give you your gifts and you can choose your date of entry and your parents, oh and of course meet your Guide. There will be lots of information to take in and we don't have much time."

"Ok Merlin, I will go and have a think, but I'm feeling I should go, what's the chances of meeting up with Jazz, Zee and Nathalie etc."

"I'll have a chat with Mother Mary and see if we can do anything, so your paths cross, however, I'm not promising anything."

"Ok, I understand, I'll see you in the morning Merlin, oh and I'm really sorry for bursting in like that, I was just shocked to see no one around."

"Have a good sleep Sophia and I'll see you tomorrow."

Sophia got up from the armchair, stretched and walked over to where Merlin was sitting, gave him a kiss on his cheek and left his room. Merlin sat back and relaxed. Woah, he thought to himself, I'm exhausted. He allowed his eyes to close and he quickly fell asleep.

The Wake Up Call

The next morning he woke feeling refreshed and he had Sophia on his mind. He must go and see Mother Mary.

Sophia woke feeling positive and refreshed. She decided to take a walk in the Cherub Garden before going to find Merlin. It felt very strange to see no one in there just walking about. She sat down under the beautiful cherry blossom tree. She had made her decision, finally she thought to herself. Her mind wandered to her friends, and she wondered how they were doing?

"Hey Sophia!" Abe shouted over to Sophia, he ran over to her.

"Abe!" Sophia replied standing up, they both hugged.

"It's so nice to see a familiar face around here," Abe smiled.

"It sure is, it's very quiet now almost everyone has left."

"So, where did you get to everyone was looking for you."

"Really? Oh I feel awful Abe, my head was hurting, I kept being asked if I was going to do the mission, and I really didn't know what to do, so I took myself off to the Sanctuary Room, I had only planned to be an hour. I fell asleep and slept almost all day, when I woke up, everyone had gone."

"Well we all searched for you, everywhere, even Mother Mary and Jazz looked in the Sanctuary Room and they said no one was there."

"Oh that's because I was tucked up in a pod, fast asleep. I feel so bad and I'm so upset, I feel I let them down."

"It's ok Sophia, they knew you wouldn't be staying away on purpose, Zee and Jazz told me to look after you, oh and Jazz said, to tell you, to get your bum on this mission, cos she needs you there." Abe said smiling.

Sophia smiled back at Abe "I have made a decision Abe, I'm going."

Abe's eyes opened wide. "You are going?"

"Yep, I'm terrified but after waking up and finding them gone, I realised I really miss them and I would rather be there with them than here, just watching, so I'm going and I hope to love I find them, then we can work together as one, rather than fighting this battle alone."

Abe dropped the corners of his mouth and nodded, "Fair play Sophia, and you know I will be right here watching you all and helping."

"Oh Abe, I couldn't do this without you watching over us all, that makes me feel safe just knowing, that you are here." They gave each other another hug.

"So now what?" Abe asked Sophia.

"Oh, well I have to go see Merlin, and let him know of my decision and then he will assist me in my departure."

"Cool, when do you go? Do you know?"

"Nope, but I know it won't be long we have limited time, he said, so I'm just appreciating what I will miss here before I go and see him."

"Ah yes, our beautiful gardens."

"Yes exactly that and I'm curious to know what's in that building over there, I've never been there, have you Abe?" she said pointing over to the Hall of Reunion, it was shaped like a dome and full of light.

Abe looked over to where she was pointing. "Nope, I can't say I have or that I've ever noticed it before."

"Mmm, I may just go and check it out," Sophia said.

"Ok well, I can't come with you because Archangel Michael is supposed to be coming over to the control room to give us some lessons. So I'll leave you to it. Safe journey Sophia and remember I'm always with you." Hugging Sophia, Abe could feel her tears rising.

"Thank you Abe." Sophia whispered and Abe squeezed her one more time and then left, leaving Sophia all alone once again in the Gardens.

Merlin had been talking with Mother Mary and was on his way to Sophia's room to see if she had made her decision, when he passed Abe in the corridor.

"Morning Abe, where are you off to in such a hurry?"

"Oh Merlin, I'm er on my way to see Archangel Michael, he is teaching this morning."

"Ah ok, yes I remember now, erm you haven't seen Sophia by any chance have you?"

"Yes, I have just left her Merlin, she is in the Cherub Gardens."

"Great thanks Abe, enjoy your lesson with Michael." Merlin said as he walked hurriedly on.

Sophia had decided to walk to the dome shaped building and check it out. As she got close to it, she heard her name being called in the distance.

"Sophia! Sophia!" Sophia turned around to see Merlin coming towards her, his arms waving in the air and his voice echoing he name through the gardens. As he got closer to her, Sophia walked towards him.

"Merlin, are you ok? Is everything alright?"

"Oh my dear, let me just catch my breath! Everything is fine."

Sophia smiled and allowed Merlin to get his breath back. "There," Merlin said letting out a sigh, "Why are you all the way over here?"

"Oh, because I saw this building Merlin, I've never seen it before and I was just curious to see what it was."

Merlin raised his eyebrows, "Oh, well you haven't seen this building before, because we haven't shown you it. We never got time to teach you anything more, because we had to call you forward for this mission. Do you want to have a look inside?"

"Do we have time Merlin, I mean I would love to but I'm aware of time."

"Of course we have enough time", Merlin said walking towards this building. "This is the Hall of Reunions AKA the Reunion Hall, this is where we all come home to, when we have come to the end of our life on Earth, we come here to be greeted by our loved ones who are waiting for us."

Merlin opened the tall heavy glass doors and they stepped inside. The whole building was filled with bright light and Sophia could just about make out people as silhouettes, walking about. "What are they doing Merlin?"

"Wait, just wait for your eyes to adjust and they you will see." Merlin replied. It took a while, but Sophia's eyes started to get used to the brightness and could now see the whole building.

"Wow, it's bigger than it looks from the outside."

"Indeed it is." Merlin said, still standing by the heavy glass doors. In front of them were gates with numbers on them, just like in the Departure Lounge, and people coming through those gates, into the arms of loved ones.

"What are these gates for Merlin, and these people? Have they just returned home? Now?"

"Yes, these people have come to the end of their Earth life and have returned home, they have to come through the gates, that have their number on it, for example if your date of exit is 5th July 1996 you will come through gate 1 as that will be the right vibration for you to enter home, but exit life."

"Do souls know their exit date Merlin?"

"For the majority of souls, yes they do know, but once on Earth, they forget. For those that don't know, they are the ones that are seen to be struggling and we call them home."

"Wow how beautiful to come home to such love Merlin!" Sophia said watching a lady walk through gate 5 into the arms of loved ones. "She was well loved by the looks of it Merlin, look how many came to greet her."

"Oh my dear Sophia, this happens when we all arrive home, there are always many to greet you."

Sophia looked over at gate 2 where a young man had stumbled out of gate 2 and his loved ones caught him. "Oh Merlin, what's happened to him?" Sophia said looking really worried.

Merlin looked over to gate 2, "Ah he has come home suddenly, he is in shock."

"Where are they taking him?" Sophia asked as they carried him towards a room.

"He will have to go to hospital for a while to recover, his soul is weak, don't worry Sophia, he will be well looked after."

"That's sad Merlin, he probably never got the chance to say goodbye to his family and friends on Earth."

"And he will probably feel like you do Sophia, so you know how that feels right now, but like you, he will find a way, to let them know he is ok and he loves them very much, but he has to recover first."

"How Merlin, how will he be able to do that?"

Merlin smiled, "See that glass door over there?" he said pointing towards the corner of the hall.

"Yes I see it just about," Sophia replied.

"Well through that door are the Dream Room and a Contact Room."

Sophia looked at Merlin blankly.

"Come, let me show you." Merlin said, taking her hand and walked towards the far end of the Hall to the glass door. As they approached the glass door, Sophia saw a crowd of people run over to gate 12, Sophia and

Merlin slowed down to observe. An elderly man came through the gate looking, lost and confused, the crowd of people gathered around him.

"Ah Sophia, watch, you are just about to witness what this love is all about."

"What's wrong with him Merlin?"

"This man had a disease on the earth called Dementia, he lost his mind, his memories, he forgot his wife, his children and grandchildren even his friends and unfortunately he has brought the disease with him, so now watch."

Sophia stared hard to see what was happening to him, and then suddenly she saw this amazing light project out of each ones heart and spread all over him and into his heart. As if by magic, this man began to stand tall and look a lot healthier and younger than when he first came through.

"Oh my, Merlin what has happened, I can see him changing before my very eyes."

"Yes they are expanding their love vibration out, all over him and they have brought him to how he used to be in his prime of life, on the Earth plane, this would usually be between the ages of 30 to 40 years old. Now he remembers who he is and the life he has just left, now he will need to go into the hospital to recover from the 'trauma'."

"Wow, what an amazing thing to do Merlin."

"Yes Sophia, and isn't it sad that the people living on Earth have forgotten how to expand their love vibration unconditionally for all life on Earth."

"Yes Merlin it is very sad." Sophia replied as she watched the crowd escort the man into the hospital.

"Come on, let me show you" Merlin said taking her hand again and leading her through the glass door. Once inside, Sophia noticed a nurse sitting at a desk, she looked up and smiled at Merlin.

"Merlin, to what do we owe this pleasure?"

"Good morning my dear, I am just showing my young recruit around and would like to show her the hospital and the other rooms, if that is ok?"

"Of course Merlin, everyone is resting and there are no emergencies at the moment, so please feel free." The nurse gave Sophia a smile and then smiled at Merlin. "Thank you my dear." Merlin smiled back and started to walk towards the double doors. Just as he got there he turned to Sophia and winked, "Ready?"

"Ready!" Sophia replied.

Merlin opened the double doors and walked through, Sophia followed behind. Sophia first noticed the man who had to be carried from gate 2. He was just sleeping and a nurse was sitting with him.

"He needs to rest." whispered Merlin.

Sophia nodded, she felt very compassionate towards him. They carried on around the hospital, seeing different souls at different stages of recovery. They came to the Room of Dreams, Merlin turned to Sophia, put his finger up to his mouth and said "Sssh, this is the Room of Dreams, this is where we can go and visit our loved ones in their dreams. We have to be extra quiet so as to not disturb them, so we won't talk while we are in there ok?"

"Yes of course." Sophia replied.

As Merlin opened the door a warm ultra violet light escaped the room, they quickly went inside and Sophia saw a row of pods, much bigger than the ones in the sanctuary, these were upright. They watched someone go in a pod, put on headphones and type the name of who they wanted to visit on some sort of pad.

The pod closed and the dreaming commenced. Merlin looked at Sophia and motioned to leave the dream room Sophia nodded. Merlin once again opened the door and they left quickly.

"That was amazing!" Sophia exclaimed.

Merlin chuckled, "I know!"

"So can you visit us on this mission via the dream room Merlin?"

"Yes of course Sophia, we all can."

"That's so reassuring to know that Merlin, it makes me feel more safe, knowing that."

"Good, I'm pleased to hear that, now do you want to see the Contact Room?"

"Sure do Merlin."

"Ok, again we cannot really talk once in there, as the messages can sometimes get mixed up and that then becomes confusing."

"Ok, so I'll just be very quiet."

"Indeed, come on."

Merlin pushed open the door and they quickly walked in. Once in the room, Sophia noticed on one side of the room was a row of tables and chairs and on the other side was similar to the dream pods, but they were slightly bigger, you could at least get 20 people in one. Although Sophia had just seen 2 people, go into one and 3 people sitting on separate tables writing.

"What happens in there Merlin"? Sophia whispered pointing over to the pods.

"That is where we try to make contact with our loved ones on Earth, Sophia, we try and link them in to our vibration, so we can let them know we are still around and love them dearly."

"Beautiful, and what are they doing then?" she asked pointing to the people at the tables.

"They are doing the same, but in a different way, and their messages may be delayed on getting to their loved ones on Earth, but they will receive the message regardless, come on, let us not disturb them anymore." Merlin opened the door and they left the room. They were now back in the Reunion Hall.

"Merlin, I'm curious, how do we hear those messages, when we are on Earth?"

"Ah well there are people on Earth who have not allowed themselves to become too Earthly and they can still link in with us and they meditate with us, and they have a relationship with us, they have remembered, where they have come from, they are the Lightworkers and they can hear the message and pass it on, when it is needed. People on the Earth, call them mediums or clairvoyants, but they also get judged and ridiculed for what they do."

"It's a cruel world, Earth, isn't it?" Sophia said sadly.

"Sometimes yes, but not always, there is still a lot of love and kindness on Earth, so don't focus on the bad things, there are good things there too."

"Mmm maybe."

Merlin chuckled, "Sophia! Don't be so negative, out of all the people, these Lightworkers have helped, it's only a few that judge and ridicule, but these people just lack the understanding of it, they are trapped in the illusion of the dark forces. These people are not bad people, they're just lost and confused, and the Lightworkers know this, and it's ok."

"Well I just feel sad, that these people cannot see."

"I don't want you to be sad Sophia, these are the people, you or the other recruits are going to help, we need them to wake up and know they have a purpose and they matter."

"I know Merlin, and now I've just remembered, my friends have gone."

"Come on, let's get out of here and have a walk in the gardens, it's a beautiful day." Merlin guided Sophia out of the building and back through the gardens, they walked for a while in silence. It was truly a beautiful day, the sun was now high in the sky and its light was reflecting a beautiful shimmer on the green leaves and the flowers.

It was warm and the smell of all the different aromas from the flowers were strong but sweet. They both walked towards the cherry blossom tree and took a seat on the bench underneath it.

Merlin was the first to speak. "You know that we don't have much time?"

"Yes Merlin, and yesterday I was feeling strong and I wanted to go, mainly to find my friends and make sure they were ok, but now I have that helpless feeling back and I'm feeling scared again, I mean, what is that all about?"

Merlin sighed, "That's the battle within, I told you about that, one is ego and the other…."

"Yes, yes, I remember that I do." Sophia interrupted.

"Well then I repeat are you afraid of giving but not getting back? Are you afraid of loving, but not being loved?"

"No Merlin, I'm not afraid of any of those, my answers have stayed the same."

"Then you will do just fine on the mission, Sophia, Courage is not because there is no fear, courage is victory over fear."

Merlin looked at Sophia and smiled. Sophia remained looking at the beautiful flowers ahead of her. After a long silence Sophia spoke, "Ok Merlin, I'm ready, I want to go and find my friends and help them achieve the mission ahead, so what do I have to do now?"

The Wake Up Call

Merlin gave her a big squeeze. "That's my girl! Right we best get on with it then, come on, we need to go to the Halls of Learning."

"Merlin, did you manage to speak to Mother Mary about me finding Zee and Jazz etc?" Sophia asked standing up and helping Merlin to stand.

"I did have a word Sophia, and we can't promise anything, but we are going to do our best to get you all together for a little while if nothing else."

"Ok, well thank you for trying, I hope we do meet up."

"Let's get a move on and get you off on your way then."

They both walked out of the gardens arm in arm. When they got to the Halls of Learning only Archangel Gabriel was there.

"Ah Gabriel, do you know where the others are, we've come to collect Sophia's gifts before she leaves."

"Oh Merlin, I'm afraid they have gone to do something else now, we didn't realise we had anyone left to see."

"Ah that's ok, we didn't know Sophia was going, she fell asleep in the Sanctuary Room and missed her time."

"Well," Gabriel said looking at Sophia who was shyly standing behind Merlin, "I still have the gifts here, so I can give them to you."

"Brilliant!" Merlin shouted making Sophia and Gabriel jump. "Ok Sophia, just follow me."

Sophia walked after Gabriel, who led her to a long table.

"Are you ok? Are you sure you are ready?" Archangel Gabriel asked Sophia.

"Yes, yes I'm ok and I'm ready to do my best, whatever happens, you are with me right?" she said looking back at Merlin.

"We are all with you always Sophia, that's a promise." Merlin smiled.

Archangel Gabriel nodded in agreement.

"Ok let's get on with this", Merlin said. Archangel Gabriel took Sophia's hand and placed a white feather in her hand.

"Normally Archangel Sandalphon would be presenting you with this gift, as you can see, it's a white feather and this will show up on Earth, whenever you are seen to be struggling or when you need a gentle reminder to let you know that we are with you always, holding you and walking with you, put it somewhere safe and know whenever it appears in your Earth life, it's a message from us, that all will be ok."

Sophia held the feather gently before putting it in her pocket. She looked at Archangel Gabriel and smiled.

"Ok the next one is the key, a key of knowledge and wisdom and this key would usually be given to you by Archangel Metatron, he is the keeper of the Akashic records, you will learn more about them, another time."

"The key will be there, whenever you are in need of knowledge, it is within you always, all you have to do is go within and trust the knowledge you receive, this you will need more than once on your path on Earth."

Archangel Gabriel placed a key in Sophia's hand, it was warm to her touch, and very solid in form although not heavy. It had a little pattern on it, at the top. She held it in her hand for a few moments before putting it into her pocket, with the feather. Once again she looked up at Archangel Gabriel and said softly, "Thank you."

Archangel Gabriel smiled and continued, "Archangel Raziel would give you a colour, your colour is silver, you will feel this colour gives you some form of protection, this will be your favourite colour on Earth, and we can link in with you via this colour, when we need to."

Sophia smiled, "Actually silver is my favourite colour, so I'm glad I have it." "Excellent, ok so the next gift is a number, this number is assigned to you, for you will need the vibration of this number to help you with your Earth life, your number is 7."

"Oh I really thought you were going to say 9, for some reason, mmm 7, I like it."

"Good, I'm glad, it sometimes takes a while to adjust to the vibration of the number, but hopefully you will be just fine, just hold the vision of the 7 in your mind for a few moments before we move on."

Sophia closed her eyes and breathed in the vibration of the number 7. She felt the vibration clear her body and for a while she thought she was floating, she opened her eyes and Merlin was smiling at her.

"You ok Sophia?"

"Yes Merlin, I just absorbed my number, I feel incredibly light."

"This feeling is temporary, you will feel like you again in a few minutes. Are you ready for the next gift?"

Sophia nodded. Archangel Gabriel continued, "The next gift, Sophia is a feeling, more than an object or a vibration."

This is the Gift of Courage and I will place this gift in your heart and solar plexus energy centre, this Gift you will need to use on many occasions during your time on Earth, when you need Courage, you will feel it."

Archangel Gabriel placed her hands on Sophia's hands and moved them on to her heart and solar plexus, and allowed the feeling of courage to pass through. Sophia closed her eyes once more and breathed in the feeling. She opened her eyes suddenly.

"Oh I think I'm already familiar with this feeling, I've had this feeling recently when I decided to commit to this mission."

Merlin chuckled, "Well Sophia, courage will be a great friend to you if you allow it to."

Sophia closed her eyes and whispered, "I will."

Archangel Gabriel dropped her hands and Sophia opened her eyes. "Ok Sophia, two more gifts, this one is hope, It will do the same as courage, place your hands on your heart energy centre. This is where your Gift of Hope will live, hope is powerful and all the time you have hope in your heart, life will never give up on you."

Sophia closed her eyes and she breathed in the feeling of Hope, it was a strong powerful feeling but with a softness to it. She opened her eyes and said, "Wow!" Merlin smiled, "Powerful huh?"

"Yes very, it nearly took my breath away!"

Merlin laughed, "Well, the next gift, will almost certainly do that."

Archangel Gabriel went on to say, "The final gift is the gift of Unconditional Love, this is truly beautiful."

Sophia closed her eyes once more and allowed the feeling of Unconditional Love to embrace her. The feeling quickly overwhelmed her, and she started to cry.

"Oh my, what a beautiful feeling, we all need to feel this." Sophia said, still with her eyes closed, through her tears.

"It is indeed Sophia, try to stay with it for a bit longer, this is the energy, the Earth people need the most."

"Merlin, it's making my heart flutter and it feels like it's thumping really fast."

"It's ok Sophia, that's just your heart getting into alignment with the vibration of Unconditional Love, just carry on breathing it in."

"Ok Merlin, will my heart stop thumping?"

"Yes of course."

Sophia opened her eyes, "Wow, that was mind blowing!"

"How does your heart feel now?"

"Oh, it feels like normal again Merlin."

"Good, it is now beating in alignment with the love vibration."

Sophia sighed and smiled.

Merlin turned to Archangel Gabriel and said, "Thank you Gabriel, for the gifts and your time, I can do the rest now."

"My pleasure Merlin, and Sophia, good luck on your journey."

"Thank you so much Archangel Gabriel." Sophia gave her a big hug.

Merlin smiled at Archangel Gabriel and she left the Halls.

"So", Sophia said turning to look at Merlin, "do I get to meet my Guide next?"

Merlin chuckled, "You are looking at him!"

Sophia stared wide eyed, "You?"

"Yes Sophia me, I decided I would be your Guide to help you on this mission."

"How can that be Merlin? You are needed for the battle on the Astral Planes, how are you going to be in two places at once?"

"I think you may have had too much sleep Sophia and have forgotten, that I am Merlin, and I can use my magic to be in two places at once."

"So never fear Sophia, I will always be with you."

"How will I know Merlin? How will I remember you are with me?"

"I will leave you signs and you will feel my energy, you will just know."

"Oh Merlin, I'm totally overwhelmed that you are going to guide me, I feel so much better."

Merlin smiled, "I'm pleased my dear Sophia, now let's sort out your date of entry." "Oh yes, can I choose a date Merlin?"

"Erm, let's have a look shall we? Remember if we want you to cross paths with Jazz and Zee, we need you around the similar age, so let's have a look at their date of entry."

Merlin opened a huge book titled Registration of Entries, he then scanned some dates, "1943, 1956, nope, 1960, 1968, wait 1968 is ok!"

Merlin went through the months in the year 1968. "February, June, July, August, aha here he is, 20th August 1968."

"Who Merlin, who's date is that?" "Zee of course, I can see his friend went earlier on the 5th August, ok let's find Jazz."

Merlin proceeded to scan the dates of 1968. "September November, December, no, mmm, did Jazz enter later?" Turning the page to 1969 and once again scanning the months of 1969. "January, March…August…September…November…aha here she is!" Merlin said pointing at a date with Jazz's name next to it.

Sophia looked closely, "The 24th November?" is that her date of entry?"

"It is indeed Sophia, so as you didn't leave the same time as them, you will have to enter December 1969 or 1970, but remember to not leave too much of a gap, you need to make sure, you make it more likely for your paths to cross."

"Mmm ok give me a minute Merlin, I need to get a feeling."

"Take your time, but please not all day!" Merlin laughed.

After a short pause Sophia spoke, "Merlin, I like the date 4th April 1970, I have a good feeling about it."

"So it is, your date of entry is 4th April 1970."

Sophia squealed, "Eek this is it Merlin!"

"Now Sophia, let's have a look at your parents."

"Oh Merlin, I was concentrating so much on my date of entry I forgot about choosing my parents."

"Well don't worry too much, because we can concentrate on them now, so let's close this book and go over to the computer pad."

Merlin closed the book shut and walked over to the computer pad. "Right Sophia, you need to choose parents that are in England, as that is where Zee and Maree are residing at present, so let's give you all every chance of meeting up."

"Ok Merlin, how about these for parents?" Sophia said pointing at a family of 6.

"No, no, you can't have that family, they are on a totally different mission to you, and their family is already complete, look it says it in the corner, family complete."

"Oh yes, I missed that, oh I'm disappointed, they look like a lot of fun and a happy lovely family."

"They are and they are doing really well on their mission, but there is plenty more keep looking."

Sophia carried on looking and then spotted a young couple, very much in love. "How about these for parents Merlin?"

"Ah yes, a young couple just starting out in life together, yes Sophia, this young couple will be perfect for you and your growth and perfect for you on this mission, you won't be an only child, a sibling will come later, but for now this is the perfect situation for you to enter."

Sophia looked at Merlin, eyes wide and said "Oh my, Merlin, I'm actually really nervous."

Merlin chuckled, "You will be fine, these parents have love, the one thing you are going to give, and they will love you very much, in their own way of course."

"Ok Merlin, well that's it then, we have finished, all that's left is for me to leave."

"Yes, have you said all your goodbyes?"

"Well I didn't get a chance to, they had already left! But I would like to get a chance to say goodbye to Mother Mary"

"And that's exactly what I've come to say Sophia!" said Mother Mary as she walked into the Hall. Sophia and Merlin, turned to see Mother Mary walking towards them. "Oh Mother Mary, I'm so pleased you came."

"Well I am pleased you have decided to go on the mission, it took you a while." Mother Mary replied raising her eyebrows.

Sophia laughed shyly, "Yes I know, but I'm still scared."

"You will be fine, Sophia, just have faith, and believe in yourself, I have no doubt, you will succeed in the job at hand."

"It's nice of you to say Mother Mary, I hope I do you all proud and we all succeed in bringing the Earth's love back into balance."

Mother Mary smiled, "Well goodbye, good luck and remember we are with you always."

Sophia gave Mother Mary a big hug, squeezed her eyes tight shut to stop the tears from falling and whispered "Thank you Mother Mary."

"Ahem" Merlin interrupted "We best get to the Departure Lounge, it's nearly time."

"Yes of course," Mother Mary replied breaking free from the hug, she squeezed Sophia's hand one last time and gave her a wink, she turned to Merlin. "I take it you will be gone, until Sophia has arrived safe and well?"

"Yes, but I will then be back to discuss the plan of action for the Astral Planes."

"Good, well safe journey both of you, take care."

"Thank you Mother Mary." Merlin and Sophia replied as Mother Mary made her way out of the Hall.

Soon it was just the two of them stood in silence looking out of the Hall, it took a while before Merlin spoke.

"Come on then, let's get you to the Departure Lounge." He held her hand and they walked out of the Hall.

Chapter Fourteen
The Wait

"Merlin, how many are there, that are on this mission?" Sophia asked as they walked down a long corridor, towards the Departure Lounge.

"It's impossible to give you an exact number Sophia, but it's more likely to be thousands than hundreds."

"And they are all on planet Earth to make a difference and bring the Earth back into balance?"

"Yes, why are you asking?"

"No reason, I'm just curious and I suppose I'm thinking."

"Well what are you thinking about?"

"I'm thinking that if there are thousands on planet Earth already, trying to succeed in this mission, how comes we are now being called?"

"Sophia, I explained all this already, you have been called, because the thousands that are already there, are being overwhelmed by the People of the Dark, and they are getting sucked into the illusion or they have forgotten about their mission and you have been called to remind them, wake them up and show them who they really are."

"Don't get me wrong, there are other souls who have gone to Earth to learn about love, to practice expanding their vibration of love outwards, they are on Earth to evolve, so not everyone you see will be on the same mission as you, they have their own mission, so their soul can grow and evolve. And may I also add some are on Earth to do both, quite a challenge for those poor souls, but they are there trying to share their light, wake others up and also to evolve themselves, for their own personal growth."

"Wow Merlin, that's a mission all by itself, to learn, grow and evolve, but to also have a mission, a purpose to help others shine, where do they get the time and energy from."

Merlin smiled, "By growing, evolving and learning, you automatically will inspire others, it cannot be any other way."

Sophia sighed, "Well I hope I succeed with everyone in this mission, but most of all, I hope to find my friends, I don't want them to feel alone or lost."

"Ah well you have to get there first, here we go, down these stairs." Merlin replied leading the way down the stairs. "You will start to feel quite heavy Sophia, this is perfectly normal, it's all about your own energy coming into alignment with the Earth's atmosphere."

"Good job you just said that Merlin, I was thinking that I felt strange."

"Go with it Sophia, it will pass."

Merlin opened the doors into the Departure lounge and Sophia took in a deep breath, her eyes wide and said, "Oh wow!"

"Quite impressive isn't it?" Merlin said softly.

Sophia just nodded, as she looked around the Lounge.

There were a few people running in different directions, some were just sitting waiting patiently, others were chatting excitedly. It wasn't as busy, as it was before when everyone left, but still busy enough for Sophia to get a sense of what her friends must have seen and how they had felt.

"Come on Sophia, let's find your gate, it's number 7, so it must be this way." Merlin started to walk away from the door and towards the gates, looking for gate 7 as he went.

Sophia followed still wide eyed and looking all around her. "How, how long has this been here Merlin? I mean how long has this existed?"

"I like that about you Sophia, don't ever stop questioning, don't ever stop asking questions. It's always been here and you have been here many times before too, you just don't remember."

"I have? Why don't I remember?"

"Well that's another long story and we need to really focus on one thing at a time, so I promise to tell you about it at another time, for now though can we just focus on the present, where we are."

"Of course Merlin, I'm sorry, it's just seems all so much to take in."

"It is my dear Sophia." Merlin carried on walking.

"Merlin!" Sophia whispered, jogging to catch him up, "Merlin!" Sophia whispered again.

Merlin stopped walking and turned to Sophia, "What's the matter Sophia?"

Sophia pointed behind her, "Who or what are they?"

Merlin looked over Sophia's shoulder to silhouettes of Light Beings.

"Oh they are the star people, they come from the Universe of Stars."

"What are they doing here Merlin?"

"The same thing as you Sophia, they have chosen to come and help planet Earth, remember Earth has a heart, they have come to help increase that love vibration."

"Oh, how are they going to do that Merlin, they are just pure light!" Sophia asked with a puzzled look on her face.

Merlin pointed to some seats. "Come sit for a minute." Once seated Merlin continued. "You are quite right Sophia, they are pure light, their vibration is so much higher than yours, that they can only be light beings, this is, I suppose, what unconditional love looks like at this high vibration."

"However, they are also aware that Planet Earth and the people on it are in trouble right now so they are choosing something that is going to be extremely hard for them to do, knowing it can be a painful experience, knowing that they may fail, they are choosing to lower their vibration to become aligned with the Earth and try and help."

"Wow Merlin, what beautiful beings of light, they are!" Sophia replied still looking at them, with kindness in her eyes now.

"Yes indeed, and although they know they could face pain, challenges and trauma, they also know this is temporary and they will return home soon. Now watch, their gate has opened, watch carefully Sophia."

Sophia stared at the queue of Light Beings, carefully, she didn't know what she was watching out for, but whatever it was, she didn't want to miss it. As the Light Beings got closer to their gate, as if by magic Sophia saw their vibration lower.

"Merlin oh my, did you see?"

"Yes Sophia, that's why I told you to watch."

"They changed as a group, they changed into elephants!"

"Yes, yes Sophia, I can see also, now watch the next group go through the gate."

"Mammals!! Merlin, Mammals!" Sophia squealed with amazement, she couldn't quite believe her own eyes.

Merlin rolled his eyes, "Yes Sophia, you are quite right, now keep watching."

The next group stepped through the gate and as they did they became birds, every species of bird you can imagine, the next group became lions and tigers.

"Wow!" Sophia exclaimed as she watched this sequence of events time and time again.

A little while after, Merlin reminded her again, "Keep watching Sophia, this group coming up will surprise you."

Sophia still in awe of what she had seen so far, looked harder at the group now approaching the gate. They looked a lively group, and more than happy to go through the gate.

"Dogs and cats Merlin!"

Merlin smiled, "Yes dogs and cats Sophia."

Sophia sat back in her seat, and sighed.

"What is it Sophia?"

"How are they going to succeed in their mission, Merlin? I mean as animals and mammals?"

"Sophia, animals and mammals are the highest expression of unconditional love, they have no knowledge of any other love, they have no "attachments" to things, people or objects, so by coming to planet earth, they can express unconditional love and teach the people how to truly vibrate out unconditional love?"

"and if the people of the Earth can hear their call, they will have succeeded in their mission, however with all of you choosing to do this mission too, there is a greater chance of waking up the People of Light, so they begin to shine too, so there will be many ways in which people will choose to express the Unconditional Love within them. Albeit through a connection with the animals and mammals or through people like yourself."

"This mission is bigger than I imagined Merlin, I, we, are just playing a very small part."

"It is huge Sophia, but it needs to be, it's not just Earth that needs help, it's the whole of our Universe, my hope is that the people of the light will wake up and begin to expand their vibration. We all have a job to do, we are all here on purpose."

"The star people who have transformed into animals, Merlin, you said they have no attachments and only know unconditional love, what does that mean?"

"The star people come from a Universe, where there is just love, and love expresses itself just by being that, love. Unconditional love means they just love with no attachments, no expectations, no conditions, and no rules. They just love no matter what, on occasions they choose to incarnate into human form, however their experience in human form, can be quite distressing and painful."

"Why Merlin?"

"Well because humans have been taught to be conditional with their love and they have attachments and expectations. They also have learnt to judge others by their own standards, so their way of loving and being loved maybe quite different to another human. Even you Sophia have made attachments."

"I have?"

"Yes, you are attached to your friends, you wouldn't have considered this mission if your friends were still here, you would have been quite happy, knowing that everything you need is with you."

"And yet, your friends leave you and you now want to go and help them. I'm not saying that's a bad thing, what I'm saying is, if you were not emotionally attached to them, you would probably have stayed here, knowing that you are enough and don't need to do anything apart from love them."

"Well of course I'm attached to them, they are my friends, we have been friends for a long time and of course I want to help them, I'm scared for them Merlin, I don't want them to get lost, I don't want to lose them."

"And I repeat Sophia that is not a bad thing, no need to get defensive. You are willing to let go of what you have here, to go help your friends, which means your attachment to your friends is stronger than what you are leaving behind."

"And that by incarnating into animals and mammals is the best form of expressing their unconditional love?" asked Sophia.

"Yes, however like I said some do choose to incarnate into humans but the experience is more challenging for them. Don't try to understand it all Sophia, I'm certain, it will all come back to you at some stage of your life on Planet Earth."

"It's not that I don't understand Merlin, I'm just trying to remember it all and don't want to forget anything."

Merlin laughed, "Well that cannot be helped, Sophia, the chances are you will forget, only to remember at a later date. Come on let's get you to your Gate number." Merlin stood and held his hand out to Sophia, she gently took it and stood up. Merlin gave her hand a squeeze.

"You will be just fine Sophia, I will be with you always". They continued to walk round the lounge to Gate 7. "It's not so busy this time Sophia, so you won't have to wait too much longer". Merlin said as they passed small queue of people, waiting at Gate 6. As they approached gate 7, Sophia noticed two young girls sitting on a bench, chatting away excitedly.

"Hello!" Sophia said.

"Hi," the girls replied in unison.

"Are you two girls going on this mission too?"

"No," replied the girl squeezing her friends arm.

"No," the other girl answered "I'm going to the Earth to learn how to become more patient, more tolerant, more compassionate, to be more empathetic and to learn the expression of true unconditional love with no judgement."

"Oh that sounds amazing and no you don't need to be on a mission, you have enough work to do."

"Ah and remember Sophia, by learning all that she will be learning, she will also be inspiring others, so in actual fact, she is helping with your mission, but in a different way." Merlin interrupted, he looked over at the girls and gave them a smile and a wink.

"So can I just ask, how are you going to learn all those things?" Sophia asked looking at the girls.

"Well I'm going to help her achieve her learning." said the girl who was squeezing her friends arm.

"Oh," Sophia replied, "and how are you going to help?"

"Well," the girl said looking at her friend, with such a lot of love in her eyes, "I'm going to be her disabled child."

Sophia took a deep sigh, "Woah, that is, well that's…."

"Love!" said the girls together.

"Yes it is love alright, wowzers, I wasn't expecting you to say that. You are one extraordinary soul!"

"Well we are all extraordinary, I'm happy to help her, she is my friend, we have had many lifetimes together and last time she helped me with forgiveness, it's the least I can do."

Merlin interrupted again "Sophia I will explain about other lifetimes, I have already promised you that, but for now, can we just focus on the task at hand."

Sophia laughed, "Yes Merlin, you know me, I ask a lot of questions."

"I knew you were going to ask about their lives together previously and we haven't got long, our gate will be open soon, I just don't want to start something, we are unable to finish."

"Understood Merlin. So have you decided if you are going to be a boy or a girl or how disabled you are going to be?"

"Yes, we've discussed everything and agreed to all we have decided on and now I'm here just to wave her goodbye and I will be back here when it's my turn to enter Earth, which here, will be in a blink of an eye, but on Earth it will be around 30 years time, take a few years before or after."

"Sorry, I don't even know your names, and hey maybe our paths will cross one day also. I hope they do and I hope I remember you."

The girl furthest away from Sophia lent forward "I'm Serena."

"And I'm Maddie and yes that would be so awesome if our paths did cross."

Serena nodded in agreement.

"I'm Sophia and this is my Guide Merlin, and I'm hoping to find my friends who have gone on this mission ahead of me."

"Well good luck and I hope you find them. Hello Merlin."

"Hello Serena, all the best in your quest, but I'm sure you won't need it, the love between the two of you will see you through the tough days and shine through the best days. I'm incredibly proud of you both and you both will be an inspiration to many, another perfect example of Unconditional Love expressing itself."

"Thank you Merlin" both girls replied. "Come on Sophia, let's not take any more time away from these girls, let us have a walk over to the bench over there." Merlin said pointing to a bench on the other side of Gate 7.

Sophia looked over to where Merlin was pointing. Sitting on the bench was a young lad, he was hugging his rucksack, staring at the floor. Sophia said bye to the girls and followed Merlin. As they got to the bench Merlin spoke, "Hey there, you don't mind if we take a seat next to you, do you?"

The young lad looked up and replied, "No not at all, please do."

Merlin and Sophia sat down. Sophia lent forward and spoke to the young lad. "Hi I'm Sophia, are you ok? You seem a little down." "No I'm ok, I'm just in my head that's all."

"Do you want to talk about it?" Merlin asked turning to look at him.

The young lad looked at Merlin and smiled. "My name is Mac, I am ok seriously, it's just I'm new to this, I've never been to the Earth before, I'm not sure I can deal with the heaviness of the Earth plane, I don't know whether to quit, and stay or take the leap of faith and go."

"Ah I see, well have you picked your parents already?"

"Yes sir, I have which is why I know I have to go, they are expecting me, but I'm not sure I can actually do it, but I don't want to disappoint them and let them down." Mac looked back down at the floor, trying to swallow the lump that had risen in his throat.

"Your parents would be ok, with whatever you decided to do Mac, they also had to choose, what they wanted to learn and experience. Maybe they chose to experience loss, and disappointment and forgiveness, sometimes it is the child that gives the gift to the parent, to allow the parent, to grow and evolve."

"Yeah I understand that, but how do I know, how do I know for sure, that is what they chose?"

"You don't, but they too would also have forgotten about what they chose, so the experience will be real to them. Or they could have chosen to help a new soul come into the world for a short time, to get used to the Earth's heavy vibration and then let the new soul return home, this may happen many times, before the new soul is ready to stay on earth."

"Wow how beautiful Merlin, what a beautiful thing to do, sacrifice your own joy to allow a new soul to adjust to the vibration of Earth."

"Sophia, once again, this is Unconditional Love expressing itself on a physical level. We are Unconditional Love, which is your mission to wake up those on Earth, who have forgotten."

Mac stood up and stretched and sat back down again. "So, you are saying that I can make the choice to go but can come home after a short while, just to allow my soul to adjust to the heavy vibration and my parents would be ok with that?"

Merlin softly smiled, "No, your parents would experience the pain of your loss, they would be heartbroken. Of course they wouldn't be ok with that. They wouldn't know why it has happened to them. However, their soul, their higher self will understand everything and their soul will know it is ok and it's ok to grieve and be utterly devastated."

"Sometimes an experience like this can wake them up to a different perspective, and they develop some understanding, which can bring comfort. Sometimes the pain remains with them and they don't recognise the experience as a gift, until they too return home."

Mac gave a big sigh, "Talking about it has made me feel worse! I mean do I give it a try and go, but come home before I enter, or do I wait enter Earth and come home or do I enter and stay for a bit, then come home, it's just so difficult."

Sophia looked at Merlin and said, "And I thought my decision was a tough one!"

"My dear Mac, you are not on your own, there are thousands of new 'Earthers' making the same choice and leap of faith as you are today, whatever, you choose to do, just remember it comes from unconditional love, ask yourself, what you want to learn and experience and what gift could you also give to your parents, what could they learn and experience to evolve, to become more enlightened. Don't analyze too much, give your mind a rest, what is your heart saying? Silence your mind, and you will hear your heart speak."

"I think I need to take some time out to listen to my heart." he said picking up his rucksack and standing up, Mac turned to Merlin. "Thanks for your insight, I really do appreciate your time." Mac then looked at Sophia and said, "And good luck on your decision to enter Earth, I hope it's successful and you keep safe."

"Thank you Mac, and maybe if you do decide to enter Earth and stay, we may bump into each other one day." Sophia replied standing up and giving Mac a hug.

Mac smiled, "Yeah maybe."

Merlin stood and took Mac's hand, "Take your time, the decision you make will be the right one."

"Thank you!" Mac replied and turned and walked away.

Sophia let out a huge sigh. "Merlin you said there was thousands of new 'Earthers' coming to Earth, is that including us, are we new 'Earthers'?"

"No Sophia, you have been to Earth many times before and have had many lifetimes, which is why the heaviness you feel in this departure lounge is bearable for you, you are adapting to the feeling quite quickly the new 'Earthers' are new souls to this level, to the Earth plane, they have never experienced any other vibration, only their own light vibration, which is why their transition can be a difficult one."

"So this can be the reason for Mac not knowing what to do?"

"Exactly, you see the new 'Earthers' are also coming forward to share their vibration, to help the Earth's heart to raise the vibration, to bring the Earth back into balance, we are all connected, we are all here to help each other, not destroy each other."

"Wow, this mission is much much bigger than I thought, it's more of a Universal Mission Merlin."

Merlin smiled "Yes it is indeed universal Sophia and possibly bigger than you can imagine."

"Mmm I wonder what Mac will decide to do?"

"Well whatever he decides to do, he will change the lives of others, that's for sure."

"That's a scary thought Merlin."

"Yes but whatever you choose to do, will also change the lives of others, in fact everybody who has made a choice, will have consequences that will change the lives of others, it is down to the others, to choose how to react and that then changes the lives of others etc. It's a cycle."

"So you are saying my choice will change the lives of others?"

"Yes!"

"I have that power?"

"Everyone has that power Sophia, they have just forgotten about their power and yes both for good and bad, your choices will change the lives of others."

"Mmm, I'm not sure that I'm totally understanding what you are saying Merlin."

"I'm not sure I'm going to have enough time to explain it, but ok, let me try and explain."

"And I, Merlin, will do my best to understand what you mean."

"Ok let's start with Mac, Mac just say for arguments sake, decides not to come to Earth, therefore his choice will result in the parents having to experience a miscarriage, this experience will change their lives in one way or another, the grief may be too much too bear and the relationship falls apart or they go on to never have children, but they are such a strong couple they foster or adopt, or they do something for charity, their choices are endless but their choices have been the result of Mac's choice."

"Another example is if you decide to leave your current job and look for another job, that decision will change the life of another person who will take your place in your old job. You see something so small like leaving your job can change another person's life, it's all about understanding the cycle."

The Wake Up Call

"Once you are aware of the effect your choices can make to others, you can then decide if you make a choice from love or not. This is why you have been called on this mission, to show people, they have a power within, the power of love."

"I think I get it Merlin, everything we do or every choice we make affects others a bit like the ripples on the pond, after you throw a stone, and we are totally responsible for our own choices that we make, nobody else has the power to make us do or feel anything. However, we need to be aware of our choices because every choice has a consequence that we alone have to be responsible for."

"Brilliantly put Sophia, that is exactly right, the challenge is to remember that always and be aware of the choices you make." Merlin winked.

They sat in silence for a few minutes. A voice from Gate 7, brought them back, brought them back, from their thoughts.

"Gate 7 will be open in 3 minutes, please make your way to Gate 7!" A small group of people started walking towards gate 7.

"So this is it Merlin, we are very nearly on our way."

"Indeed Sophia, not long now." Merlin replied standing up.

Sophia followed, stood up and stretched. "Will this heaviness get better Merlin, once we go through the Gate?"

"You will feel pressure at the top of your head as you enter Earth Sophia, but once you enter your body will have adjusted to the heaviness of Earth and you will feel just fine. Now let's get you in this queue."

"Ok Merlin."

Soon they were the next to go through the Gate.

"Ready Sophia?"

"No, but yes!"

"You will be ok, and remember I am always with you."

"Sophia, you're next sweetheart said the Gate Keeper.

"Ok I'm here. Merlin I am doing the right thing aren't I?" she said holding his hand.

"Absolutely Sophia, and I'm with you, all the way."

Sophia smiled, squeezed Merlin's hand, and stepped forward, feeling immense pressure on her head and a beautiful light as she stepped through the Gate.

Chapter Fifteen
Destiny

Sixteen years later, Merlin calls for a meeting with Mother Mary, to discuss Sophia and her mission on the Earth Plane. Mother Mary knocks on Merlin's door and opens it slightly. "Hello, Merlin are you there?"

"Yes, ah Mother Mary do come in, I'm so glad you made the time to see me, I know we have such a lot going on at the moment, what with the mission on Earth and the battle on the Astral Planes, but thank you, for coming."

"It's ok Merlin, I know you wouldn't have called me, if it wasn't important, so what is it?"

"Well as you know, I've been with Sophia, gently guiding her through life on Earth, for the last 16 years."

"Yes and you said she was coping well, albeit a little introverted and having attached herself to horses?"

"Indeed, and she has been doing really well she is very observant, sees things differently, and is loving, kind and caring, and she is only 16 years old."

"So what's the problem Merlin, it sounds to me like everything is going to plan?" "Well erm, you see, well that's what I thought too, but she now has a boyfriend and that's fine, but she has really committed herself to her horses, and she has been offered to go to Germany to work in a professional show jumping yard, and she is really excited about it."

Mother Mary looked at Merlin with a blank look on her face. "And Merlin"?

"Well, I would have thought the boyfriend would have been a great distraction to keep her in the UK, but it appears not. And if she does indeed go to Germany, she may not get to find her friends, because they are in the UK."

"Ah yes, their paths will not cross."

"No and to be honest with you, I think Sophia, may have forgotten about her mission and we need to remind her of her true purpose."

"Mmm, and you believe she is not aware at all, not even subconsciously?"

"Yes, Mother Mary, I think she has completely forgotten, or she is hiding away from the task and using the horses love to express her own love, but we need to give her a wake up call, remind her of why she is here."

"Oh I see, ok, well what can we do to prevent her from leaving for Germany?"

"I don't know Mother Mary, which is why I called for this meeting with you."

"It will have to be something that stops her taking that path towards the show jumping and horses."

"Yes but what exactly can we do, to stop her for a long time, it's no good to stop her going for six months, because she will go later, I know how she feels about the horses and what she wants to do for a career. She is passionate about them Mother Mary".

"Have you tried to visit her Merlin, in her dream state?"

"Yes lots of times, but it's not waking her up, she puts it down to just a dream or night terrors, me? A night terror!" Merlin replied with a chuckle.

"Oh Merlin, this is not funny, what can we do?"

"Exactly why I called you Mother Mary." They were silent for a bit.

"What are her family like Merlin?"

"Er they are a good family, they are close and the grandparents love Sophia too."

"So they would be supportive?"

"Yes they are very supportive now, they are supporting Sophia's decision to go to Germany and they are supportive of her younger brother too."

"So they have love and support?"

"Yes, Mother Mary, what are you thinking?"

"Well it's the only way I can see, and it still may not work."

"What is it?"

"Sophia becomes pregnant, but doesn't know she is pregnant until she goes into labour. She has a boyfriend, it's feasible."

"Oh my, Mother Mary!" Merlin replied putting his hands up to his face. They both fell silent, thinking to themselves. "It could work", Merlin said after a pause. "It might backfire, her family may go mad, or adopt the baby, so Sophia can still go and do the work in Germany."

"It is a gamble indeed, because whatever happens, she will still have free will and the freedom to choose." Merlin sighed.

"Well it's the only way I can think of, I just don't see another way." Mother Mary replied.

Merlin stood up and got a glass of water. "Do you want a glass of water Mother Mary?"

"Yes please Merlin."

Merlin poured two glasses of water and sat back down. Mother Mary took a gulp of water and placed the glass on Merlin's wooden table.

"We need to try, we cannot allow her to not remember why she is there, can you imagine Sophia coming home and us then telling her that she got sucked into the illusion of life and she forgot why she was there, she would be absolutely heartbroken and her greatest fear would come true."

"What was her fear Merlin, refresh my memory."

"That she would fail, Mother Mary."

"Oh yes of course!" Mother Mary said quietly. "Well then, she can't come home to discover that and then find out, we also didn't try to put her back on the path of the mission, so let's go ahead, let her get pregnant, an accidental pregnancy."

"Yes I agree, and fingers crossed it's the right decision for her." Merlin replied.

"Who is left here Merlin? Who can we ask to do this mission? The mission of helping Sophia get back on the right path, which soul will be suitable to be Sophia's son or daughter?"

"I'm not sure, I will have to check my list, hang on, it's here somewhere."

"We need to find someone who is willing to go to Earth soon, we need to act fast Merlin."

"Well there are a few here, Rachael is here and she is strong enough to do this mission."

"Ok Merlin, let's call her in and ask her."

"I'll see if Abe can get her, he will know where to find her. I will be back in a minute Mother Mary." Merlin said as he opened the door.

Mother Mary sat back in her chair and sighed. This is complicated, she thought to herself.

Merlin found Abe sitting in the Great Halls of Knowledge.

"Ah Abe, I'm glad I found you."

"Merlin, er you were looking for me?"

"Yes, could you find Rachael for me and ask her to meet me and Mother Mary in my room?"

"Yes of course, she is with the others in the Hall of Learning."

"Ah I knew you would know where to find her, brilliant thank you Abe."

"Merlin, can I ask, is everything ok?"

"Yes and no, well it's Sophia, it appears that she has forgotten her mission and we need to now push her back on her path, which is why we need Rachael."

"Oh no I'm sorry to hear that Merlin what about the others?" Abe asked.

"Well I believe the others are all on track, apart from a few blips, but yes that's going to be expected, but I feel if Sophia doesn't get on her path, we may lose her friends too."

"What a worry Merlin, she will be devastated, when she comes home, to find that she had indeed lost her friends and her own self."

"Yes I know, which is why we need to do something Abe, so can you go and collect Rachael as soon as you can."

"Yes Merlin, I'll go right now."

"Thank you Abe, see you again soon."

Abe walked out of the Great Halls of Knowledge, Merlin stayed for a while, looking out of the huge window, where Sophia would often sit.

"I hope this is the right thing to do for you my dear Sophia." Merlin whispered.

Abe entered the Halls of Learning and spotted Rachael, straight away standing with a group of friends, they were all discussing their task that they had been set. He walked over to them.

"Hey Rach!" Abe said. Rachael looked over to Abe, "Yes I called you!" Abe said and smiled.

Rachael walked over to Abe, "What's up?"

"Merlin and Mother Mary want to see you, it's important." Abe replied.

"I haven't done anything wrong, why do they want to see me?"

"It's not because you have done anything wrong, they need to just talk to you."

"Oh!" Rachael replied somewhat puzzled at what they could want to talk to her about.

Just then River walked over to them. "Hey what's going on? Is everything ok?"

River was Rachael's best friend and he loved her, he was always there for her. They did have feelings for each other but both of them were too shy to tell each other. "I've been asked to go see Merlin and Mother Mary they want to talk to me?"

"Why what have you done?" River chuckled.

"Shut up Riv, I haven't done anything!"

"Well go and see what they want, come back and tell me yeah."

"Ok, be back in a bit."

"Come on, I'll walk you there" Abe said.

Merlin just got back to his room and Mother Mary was just making a cup of tea. "Ah Merlin, I hope you don't mind, I helped myself, would you like one."

"Not at all Mother Mary and yes please I could do with tea, Abe is on his way to get Rachael so they won't be long."

"Good, I've been thinking, while you've been gone, and I really can't think of another way forward, and it does sound as this way is the only way, but I can't help but feel it's a bit harsh for her."

"I know what you mean Mother Mary, I feel the same, but apart from giving her a heart attack at the age of 16, I don't know what else to do to wake her up."

"Yes and we may need the heart attack at a later date, if this doesn't work." Mother Mary winked and smiled, passed Merlin his tea. A knock at the door, stopped their conversation and Mother Mary answered the door.

"Ah Rachael, thank you for joining us, thank you Abe for bringing her over, do come in."

"Mother Mary I got some work to do, so can I just leave Rachael with you?" Abe asked.

"Yes, yes of course, come in Rachael, Abe thank you again, we will see you soon." "Ok great, see you later."

Mother Mary closed the door and collected her tea. "Rachael, would you like a drink or a tea?"

"No thank you Mother Mary."

"Come, sit, Rachael and don't be nervous, you have not done anything wrong, relax!" Merlin said softly.

Rachael sat in Merlin's big chair and she too realised it was more comfortable than it looked.

Merlin continued, "The reason for Mother Mary and I wanting to talk to you, is because one of our recruits who is on Earth has a mission to do, however she has forgotten all about it and we fear we may lose a really strong recruit, so to stop her from getting lost in life, as such, we need her to get back on her path." Merlin and Mother Mary looked at Rachael softly.

"Erm I'm guessing you somehow want me to help, but I don't know how I would fit in?" "Well", Mother Mary said "Merlin and I were trying to think of a way to put her back on her path and the only way we can think of is if she has a baby and that hopefully will be enough to keep her, where she needs to be for the time being".

"And you are wanting me to be that baby?"

"Yes," Mother Mary replied looking over at Merlin. "Rachael, you don't have to do this, but we know that you have been a little bored here and thought that you would like the challenge. And also you are very much like Sophia, you are strong and won't get sucked into illusions and we will always be with you."

Rachael looked at them both, she had indeed been feeling bored, if it wasn't for River, there wouldn't be any reason to stay, she had grown so much over the past five years. A little rumble of excitement made her tummy flip.

"Ok, you are right I am bored, but I don't know whether I want to actually leave River behind, can I think about it?"

"Of course," Mother Mary replied, "But you only have two hours, as we need to do this sooner rather than later and if you decide not to, then we will need to find someone else."

"Ok, I just want to talk it over with River."

"Then go, meet you back here in two hours."

Rachael got up out of Merlin's comfy chair and let herself out. Mother Mary and Merlin looked at each other and said in unison "She'll do it!" They laughed.

Two hours later Rachael came back to Merlin's room. She knocked on his door. "Come in!" Merlin shouted out.

Rachael opened the door and went inside.

"Come, take a seat." Mother Mary said.

Rachael took herself straight back over to Merlin's comfy chair, and sat herself in it.

"So have you managed to make a decision?" Merlin asked.

"Yes I have and after chatting with River, he said I should go too, it's an opportunity I cannot miss, even if it scares me to death."

"Excellent, River is a wise old soul and you don't know, he may choose to join you at a later date." Merlin said.

"Funny, he actually said that he may join me later."

"Ah you see he already knows. Ok well we need to get you prepared you need your gifts, your guide, your date of entry and well you already know your parents."

Mother Mary interrupted, "Merlin, I'll take her through it all, shall we meet you in the Departure Lounge say in an hour?"

"Yes excellent, that will give me a chance to notify Archangel Gabriel that the gates need to be lowered for a short while, and put Abe and the others on standby, we are going to be vulnerable for attack once more."

"Ok good, ready Rachael? No time like the present."

"Yes Mother Mary, take me to meet my Guide and receive my gifts, before I change my mind". Merlin chuckled "You really remind me of Sophia, I think you will be just fine."

They all left Merlin's room.

An hour later and Mother Mary and Rachael were in the Departure Lounge, sitting by Gate 11, waiting for Merlin.

"Well here we are Rachael, I know you are nervous, I can feel your energy from here." Mother Mary smiled and squeezed Rachael's hand. "Ah and here comes Merlin."

Rachael looked up and saw Merlin walking over to them.

"Hello you two, is everything ok?"

"Yes everything has gone very smoothly, hasn't it Rachael?"

"Yes I love my gifts Merlin, and although I'm nervous, I feel so much better knowing you are all watching over me and helping, I'm a little anxious that my mum, Sophia, has no idea I'm coming. What if this plan doesn't work and I get rejected by her?" "My dear Rachael, if you do get rejected by her, we will put in place replacement parents who will love you just the same, have no doubt about that. I very much doubt this will happen, knowing Sophia, she will not be able to part with you."

"I hope so Merlin." Rachael whispered.

"How much longer Merlin until Rachael can go?"

"Well it's the beginning of April on Earth and Rachael's date of entry is the 27th April so not too long." Merlin replied. "Sophia is getting a bit concerned about the weight she has put on and is trying to lose some weight, but his won't cause you any harm Rachael, you will be safe."

"You nearly had me going there Merlin, I thought you was going to say, she was thinking she could be pregnant!"

Merlin chuckled, "No, no she still has no idea, it will come as a shock, but once everyone is over the shock all will be well."

Mother Mary smiled at Merlin. She loved his optimism. They all fell silent for a while. The Departure Lounge was empty apart from the three of them, some late comers, may come later, but for now they all appreciated the silence. Merlin stood up, stretched and gave his hands a rub.

"I could feel myself nodding off, sitting there!" he said. Mother Mary and Rachael giggled, they both heard a little snore from Merlin five minutes earlier.

"I just want you to know I will be with you too Rachael, I know I'm Sophia's Guide, but you will see me in your dreams too, I will be there for you, I just needed to tell you that."

A voice on the speaker interrupted Merlin, "Gate 11 will be open in five minutes, please make your way to Gate 11!"

"That's us!" Merlin said.

Mother Mary stood up and held Rachael's hands. "This is where I say goodbye, but before I do, I want to thank you for doing something quite brave, I am very proud of you and I know you will be just fine."

"Thank you Mother Mary, I hope I can help Sophia remember her path and I continue to make you proud."

Mother Mary hugged her and whispered, "Good luck!" Mother Mary then turned to Merlin and said, "So I guess I won't be seeing you for a while, I'm sure you will be wanting to stay until the shock disappears and Rachael is settled?"

"Yes Mother Mary, although I don't think it will take long, what is there not to love about Rachael?"

"I will be back soon, we need to make a start with planning a solution to this battle on the Astral Planes."

"Indeed Merlin, we cannot leave it much longer."

"Ow, Mother Mary my head, it's starting to hurt owie! I have intense pressure on my head, what's happening?"

"Oh that's Sophia, she is in labour, ok, this may be a quick entry, ok, look Gate 11 is starting to open, come on my dear, this is all perfectly normal, try not to panic."

"Merlin, look after her!" Mother Mary said as she watched them both walk quickly towards the gate.

"I will, I promise Mother Mary."

"Merlin, it's really getting tight, are you ow! Are you sure I will be ok." Rachael asked now holding her head in her hands.

"I promise Rachael, you will be fine, this won't last long." They both walked through Gate 11 together, a flash of light and they were gone.

Chapter Sixteen
The Wake Up Call

Sophia opened her eyes slowly, she found herself in a strange room, the window and curtains were unfamiliar to her, she turned over to her other side and there facing her was a baby sleeping peacefully in a crib next to her. Sophia closed her eyes quickly, and then opened them again, and then the events of the early hours of the morning came back to her.

"Oh, and there I was thinking it was all a dream!" Sophia whispered to herself. Merlin was standing by the window, he smiled, Sophia couldn't see him, but he had been with her all through night. A soft gentle knock on the door and a midwife poked her head around the door.

"Ah you're awake, I've just come on my shift, and you and little one here have been the talk of the place, so I thought I'd come and introduce myself, my name's Alison and I'm here to look after you and little one."

Sophia smiled, "I'm so tired and I think I'm in shock, I thought this was all a dream!" Alison chuckled, "Well you won't be the first and you certainly won't be the last." "Yes but I had to idea, I was even pregnant, I didn't have a bump, nothing."

Alison smiled and plumped up Sophia's pillows and helped Sophia sit up. "Like I said you won't be the last, it's quite common you know."

"It is?" said Sophia even more surprised.

"Yes, it is not unusual."

"Wow, I thought I might be some sort of freak, you know, it's a bit weird."

"Ah you are no freak, but I understand the shock, my colleagues tell me your Mum and Nan were here, and they will be up later."

Sophia slid back down the bed with a groan, "Oh I've let them down!"

"Ah don't be daft, they will come round, just you wait and see, a new baby is never bad news, she was clearly meant to be here, once the shock of it all starts to fade, you will all be smitten, she is gorgeous." Alison said looking down at the baby. Sophia looked at her baby too, but felt numb.

"She will be due a feed soon, do you want me to take her and give her a feed and change her so you can get some sleep, before your mum comes?" Alison asked. "That would be lovely Alison, if you are not too busy out on the ward?"

"No, it's quiet at the minute, but that can change as quick as that, as you well know Sophia, but for now I will take her, you get some rest." Alison walked over to the crib and wheeled her baby out of the room.

"Thank you!" Sophia whispered.

Alison smiled and shut the door gently. Sophia sunk back into the bed, a hundred and one thoughts whizzing through her head, but the one question that kept repeating itself was, what am I going to do? Sophia fell back to sleep.

Merlin walked over to her bedside, he watched her sleeping for a while, before he spoke, "It seems to me that, that question repeats itself quite a bit".

Sophia became aware of someone speaking, she also became aware of being as light as a feather. She opened her eyes and sat up on the side of her bed, she stared out of the window for a bit and then Merlin spoke once again.

"So what are you going to do?"

Sophia looked round towards to the end of her bed and said "I'm dreaming, I've got to be dreaming!"

"No you're not dreaming, you are having what is called an out of body experience."

"A what? Who are you?" Sophia said before thinking, who the hell am I talking to, this is a dream.

"I'm Merlin, I'm your Guide, I've been with you all your life, and I've had to take you out of body, so I can talk to you and you will remember."

"Erm, I'm not out of my body, I'm very much in my body thank you!"

"Just have a look back on the bed."

Sophia turned her head to where she had been laying. "Woah, that's me asleep!" But I'm here awake, oh my God, have I died, am I dead?" Sophia exclaimed.

"No, no," Merlin chuckled, "You are not dead, you are just out of body like I told you."

"So this is just a dream, yes? I'm dreaming, deep breaths, I'm going to wake soon!"

"Sophia, you are not dreaming, you are very much awake, and I need you to listen to me very carefully, I needed you out of body, because I need to remind you of things and you need to remember."

"Sophia? You called me Sophia, that's not my name are you sure you have the right person, er Merlin, you did say that was your name right?"

"Yes my name is Merlin and Sophia is your name, just not your Earth name."

"Do you know Merlin, I have no idea what you are talking about, can you just put me back in my body, so I can wake up from this, this nightmare!!"

"No, I can't do that yet, you need to listen to me, this if you like is your wake up call."

"Well it's not working Merlin, because clearly I'm still asleep!" Sophia replied pointing towards her sleeping body.

Merlin laughed, "Sophia, please just hear me out!"

"It's not funny Merlin, do you know I've just given birth to a baby and I didn't even know I was pregnant?"

"Yes Sophia, I do and I have to own up to admitting that was the plan."

"Eh? You say you are my Guide and yet gave me no warning to prepare me for a baby?"

"Now, now Sophia, just listen I had to do something drastic you were going the wrong way, I had to do something."

"I still have no idea what you are talking about Merlin, it has been a strange 36 hours, are you sure I'm not dreaming?"

"No you are definitely not dreaming, now let me explain, before you came to Earth, we were living in another dimension and vibration, you were very happy there, with all your friends, learning how to evolve and gaining wisdom and knowledge etc." "This all sounds a little cuckoo Merlin, does it get better?"

"Just keep listening, anyway where was I, ah yes right, but what happened was the Dark Forces were coming closer to earth and earth was in serious trouble, still is to be honest with you, anyway Mother Mary and I decided we needed to do something to help the Mother Earth, so we called on you guys, our young recruits to come to Earth on a mission to bring Earth back into balance."

Sophia continued to listen and Merlin carried on telling Sophia about her purpose and the love vibration and Earth's heartbeat.

"But you didn't know whether to come Sophia, but your friends tried to find you to say goodbye but couldn't find you anywhere, so they had to leave, and you were devastated, when you found out. You then made the decision to come and do the mission, but also find your friends and let them know you are back with them."

Merlin paused, Sophia stayed silent, trying to take in all the information.

Merlin continued, "However, once you entered Earth, you fell in love with animals, horses especially and you poured your love into them and lost the reason why you are here."

"Which is to find my friends, and spread love and remind others to shine too." Sophia whispered looking at Merlin with tears in her eyes.

"Yes, yes! Sophia do you remember?" "It sounds familiar Merlin, but so far away." "Well we had to stop you going to Germany and being with horses, we had to give you a big wake up call, so you stayed here, and finally meet up with your friends and others who are also on this mission." Merlin explained.

"But a baby Merlin? Do you have any idea? I mean I'm only 17 years old! My parents, my grandparents, my life, Oh Merlin!" Sophia started to cry.

"My dear Sophia, I know this is a huge shock, to you and your family, but it will get better, I promise, and you still have a choice?"

"What choice do I have now Merlin, I'm stuck with a baby and I'm probably a huge disappointment to my family, I've let them down."

"Well you were sensible Sophia, it's not like you were stupid or anything, you have a steady boyfriend and you were both responsible, plus you didn't know this baby was coming and she is beautiful Sophia."

"Do you know her Merlin? Does she come from the same place as us?"

"Yes Sophia, she chose to come to help you stay on your mission, however, like I said you can choose to not do this mission, have your baby adopted and carry on the life you had planned out for you. There is a couple who are childless and will love her just as much as you can."

"The choice is yours Sophia, it always is, but you must try to understand that I had to remind you of the mission, because I didn't want you to come home and be disappointed that you didn't help and also angry that we didn't try to wake you up. You wouldn't have forgiven me."

"I know what you are saying Merlin and as you are saying it I believe it, but then I'm now thinking am I just making all this up?"

"I know how hard it is for you Sophia, it's a shock and lots of information to take on board. You have time, ten days in fact, as you will be given a choice to keep your baby or give her up."

"What's her name Merlin?"

"Well you need to choose a name Sophia."

"No, you know what I mean, what's her name?" Sophia now getting annoyed.

"Ah well her name is Rachael, spelt with an ael not el."

"Rachael, I like it!" Sophia smiled. "This is all still quite surreal to me Merlin, I mean I'm out of body, talking to my Guide, after giving birth to a baby girl, when I didn't even know I was pregnant, I mean really?"

"It does sound surreal when you put it like that Sophia, but in our world, anything is possible."

"So let me just get this straight in my head, if I choose to stay and be a mum to my baby, my friends will cross my path and we will all know, we are on a mission, and we have some serious work to do."

"Well your friends may not remember they are on a mission of light, vibrating their love out to others, but together you will be guided to help others shine their light." "Can I ask another question Merlin?"

"Always ask questions Sophia, question everything."

"You've said that before haven't you Merlin?"

"Not in this lifetime, but where we were before yes."

"Mmm, so my question is, how do we know who to help, how do we get this message out there?"

"People will come Sophia, they will feel your love, people will come, never mind about how to get the message out there, you will find a way, this if you choose it, is just the beginning."

"And Merlin, when I'm back in my body, you will still be with me yes?"

"Yes I have never left your side Sophia."

"But I won't be able to see or hear you?"

"Correct, although you may hear me occasionally, and you will feel my love."

"If you choose to do this mission, in time you will find light workers who are already on this mission and they will help you and then you could eventually see me."

"How will I find these Lightworkers Merlin?"

"All in good time Sophia, for now you have to choose first, it has to be your own choice."

"Rest for a while, your body needs to rest and recover from the shock, you have plenty of time."

"Ok Merlin, can I go back to my body now?"

"Yes of course, and we will speak again soon."

Sophia laid back down on the bed and fell back to sleep, shortly after she heard Merlin's voice, "So what are you going to do?"

Sophia sat up quickly, looked back at her pillow and was relieved she didn't see herself sleeping. A gently knock on the door, and Alison brought the baby back in.

"She's been as good as gold, she's been fed and changed and has now settled back to sleep."

"Thank you Alison, I've had a sleep and feel a lot better." Sophia replied.

"Good, well just relax for a bit, little one shouldn't cause you too much bother for a while, would you like to eat some lunch?"

Sophia didn't even notice that she hadn't eaten anything since lunch the day before.

"I am feeling a bit hungry, so yes please."

"No bother, I'll sort some out for you."

"Thank you Alison." Once again Sophia was left alone with her thoughts and her baby.

"Merlin!" Sophia whispered "Are you there?"

Merlin was standing by the window, "Of course I'm here but I doubt you can hear me."

"See nothing, I'm going bleeding mad and now I'm even talking to myself!" Merlin chuckled.

"Did I just hear you laugh Merlin?" Merlin rolled his eyes, and walked over to her and expanded his vibration. "Oh my, I can actually feel you Merlin! I think anyway. Or am I just imagining this?"

Alison knocked and walked in with a sandwich a packet of crisps and a yoghurt. "Here now, see how you get on with eating this."

"Oh thank you Alison, I'm sure I will eat the lot, I'm starving!"

"Ok well give me a shout if you need me, I think we have two ladies just gone into labour, but I think they will take a while."

"Oh dear, well good luck to them."

Alison quietly closed the door as Sophia started to eat her lunch. While finishing the last of her crisps, Sophia started to think it must have all been a dream, or the side effects of the medication, the doctors had to give her. She started to feel a bit more like herself, now she had eaten. She was dreading her parents coming, she felt quite sick thinking about it.

"I'll just tell them, I didn't know I was pregnant and I want to have the baby adopted and go back to doing what I was doing, and make them proud of me again." Sophia said out loud.

Merlin sighed and shook his head. He went back to tell Mother Mary the news.

"Ah Merlin, is everything ok?" Mother Mary asked as Merlin appeared in the Great Halls of Knowledge.

"Well yes and no Mother Mary, which is why I need some advice on what else to do." Mother Mary closed her book she was reading and sat up in the chair.

"What's happened?" Merlin sat down in a chair opposite Mother Mary.

"Well Rachael arrived safe and well, although a very big shock to Sophia and her family, but both are doing very well."

"That's good to hear, but I hear a but Merlin?"

"Yes indeed a but! I managed to get Sophia out of dream state and I pulled her out of her body so she could hear me and see me."

"Oh I see, well how did she take it?"

"She was confused and thought she was dreaming, however, I told her this was a wake up call, and I tried to give her as much information as I could. She listened, and at times I believed that she started to remember. Anyway, I then let her rest and go back to sleep."

"So what's happened Merlin?"

"Well she woke up, and tried to hear me and see me, and obviously she couldn't so now thinks it was a dream or she was imagining it all due to the medication etc. And before I thought it will all come back to her, she said out loud that she was going to tell her parents that she wants the baby adopted and go back to what she was doing and make her parents proud of her again, because she feels she has let them down."

"Oh dear Merlin, this is not good at all!"

"I know which is why I've come back is there anything else we can do?"

"Has Sophia not bonded with the baby yet?"

"No, she hasn't held her or fed her yet, the midwives are doing that to help Sophia recover from the trauma."

"Ok, well Sophia needs to hold her, feel a connection or something, so go back and make sure Sophia gets the opportunity to hold her baby, and if you have to Merlin, have another go at talking to her again, out of body if you have to."

"Great, thank you Mother Mary, I'm on my way."

"Take care Merlin."

While Merlin was talking with Mother Mary Sophia's parents had visited. They were in a lot of shock, but Sophia's mum was already in awe of this tiny bundle, as were Sophia's grandparents. Sophia spoke to them about giving the baby up for adoption. They told her, this was a decision she needed to make on her own, although secretly they were planning on keeping the baby in the family somehow, but had to wait for Sophia's final decision.

By the time Merlin got back to Sophia, it was night time and Sophia was sleeping, and the midwives had once again taken the baby to allow Sophia to rest. Merlin decided to try to talk to her again.

"So what are you going to do Sophia?" Sophia opened her eyes, she thought she heard a voice, she sat up.

"So what are you going to do?" Merlin repeated.

"I thought I heard something, am I dreaming again, or is that really you Merlin."

"No you are not dreaming, it's really me Merlin."

"I can't see you."

"No because you are actually awake, but you can hear me, and I'm just by the window, I'll never leave you Sophia, whatever you decide to do, it was my promise."

"Did I promise to come to Earth and help with this mission Merlin?"

"No you made a choice Sophia not a promise."

"Phew that makes me feel a bit better, I don't like to promise things and then not do what I promised."

Merlin smiled, "You haven't changed Sophia, you are still that beautiful, caring loving Sophia, life here hasn't changed you."

Sophia thought for a bit. "It's a hard decision Merlin, I mean it sounds a bit weird, doesn't it. I've chosen to come to Earth on a mission, to help others shine their light, to bring the Earth back into balance, I mean who is going to take me seriously or they might decide I've gone mad, and take me to the nearest hospital."

Merlin laughed, "Sophia, this is a hard decision, but you already made it by coming to Earth. You had already decided. You then just forgot and we have had to remind you, and you don't need to tell everyone that you are here on a mission. You just need to help others, give them hope, show them love, your action alone is this mission".

"I'm really scared Merlin, I've never done anything like this before, I mean I'm only 17 years old."

"You were scared before you came here my dear Sophia, so don't allow fear to stop you."

"What if I get laughed at or ridiculed?"

"Will that stop you from caring and loving?"

"No of course not, I'm just not sure I will like the feeling it will give me."

"You can control your feelings Sophia, don't allow them to control you."

"I am really scared Merlin."

"I will be with you always Sophia, you will be fine, you will help others shine."

"Merlin, will I recognise any of my friends?"

"Maybe not at first, but in time you will, first things first, find some light workers to help you on your path, they will help you to not be afraid."

"Oh Merlin, I need more time, I am frightened, this is a huge shock, I need to think, I just don't know what to do."

"My dear lovely Sophia, I feel like deja vue again, you were like this before you made your decision to come, take your time, I'm here always."

Sophia laid back into her bed, pulled the covers over herself and fell back into a deep sleep. Merlin sat beside her bed and quickly dozed off too.

Sophia came round to the baby quietly crying, it was 7.10am and Sophia knew she must be due a feed. Sophia got out of bed and went to find a midwife on the ward. The ward was pretty empty, but there seemed a lot of noise coming from two labour rooms. A midwife came out of one of the rooms, just as Sophia's baby started to cry a little louder.

"Oh can you help?"

"Sorry Sophia, it's gone a bit crazy here, if you need a bottle, they are in the kitchen, there should be three on the side ready to go so just take one of them."

"Ok thanks." Sophia walked into the kitchen and sure enough there was three bottles, Sophia took one, and headed back to her room, where by now the baby was really crying.

"Hey, it's ok, hungry one, it's coming!" Sophia gently said as she picked up the baby and carried her as she climbed into the bed. Cradling her gently and holding her head, Sophia looked at her for the first time properly. She really was perfect. It didn't take long before the baby started to drink her milk.

While looking at the tiny bundle, she heard Merlin say, "She chose to come and help you to get back to the mission."

"I know." Sophia whispered.

The baby then moved her hand as she was drinking her milk, she held onto Sophia's finger tightly. Sophia started to cry. "Ok ok, I will do it, I don't know how I'm going to do this mission, but I will do it, I promise."

Merlin let out a huge sigh of relief. He rushed back to let Mother Mary know. Sophia held her baby, and cried, somehow the baby seemed to squeeze Sophia's finger a little tighter.

Just then Sophia's mum walked in and looked at Sophia crying. "Oh darling, whatever is the matter?"

"Oh mum, I want to keep her!"

Sophia's mum started to cry too. "Oh that is absolutely fine darling, we will support you, whatever your decision, and we love her already, have you thought of a name for her?"

"Rachael, Mum I really like Rachael."

"A beautiful name, I'm just going to let Dad, Nan and Granddad know, I'll be back in a minute."

"Ok Mum, love you."

"Love you too darling."

Sophia was left alone once again, looking down at her baby, who was nearly finished her bottle.

"Thank you Rachael," Sophia whispered, "I love you."

"I will be ok won't I Merlin?"

"You will be just fine my dear Sophia. This is just the beginning….."

www.ingramcontent.com/pod-product-compliance
Lightning Source LLC
LaVergne TN
LVHW010300260326
834688LV00044B/1374